Syndication Nation

The Definitive Guide to Radio, TV, Internet and Print Syndication

Chris J. Witting, Jr.

Dedication

This book is dedicated to my children, John and Karen, for their love and unwavering support. I love you both very much.

Table of Contents

Acknowledgements

Many people generously provided their time and expertise to help make this book a reality. Thanks to the visionaries who provided plenty of wisdom and inspiration on the wide-ranging and fascinating topic of media syndication. In no particular order, I wish to thank Alex Paen, Cassie Yde, Jeremy Coleman, Eric Nuzum, Marvin Kempner, Kim Dushinski, Seth Godin, Ken McCarthy, Frank Kern, Dan Kennedy, Yanik Silver, Perry Marshall, John Reese, Bill Glazer, Joel Comm, Mike Filsaime, and other advisors too numerous to mention here. Thanks also to broadcast veterans Doug Stephan, Bruce Williams, Mike Carruthers, Weezie Kramer, Rick Starr, Carl Amari, and many others for their contributions to this effort.

My sincere gratitude goes to our many loyal syndication clients, hosts, and producers. Thanks to the talented management team and staff at Syndication Networks for their tireless efforts on behalf of our clients, hosts, producers, and affiliate stations.

Thanks to the nearly 2,000 stations that carry our programs and to the many millions of people who comprise our total national audience. We appreciate their responsiveness and involvement in our programs. We also acknowledge our industry partners, who have played a key role in our business growth. These include Ken Williams, David Landau, Charles Steinhauer, Tricia Anderson, Chris Birkett, Steve Silberman, Richard Gayle, and many others. I wish I had more room to list everyone here! Lastly, I am grateful to professional editor Nancy Witting who met every deadline with panache and skill; to friends and family who encouraged me to complete this project, and to my friend Guruji for his always helpful guidance. Lastly, I thank you the reader for your interest in syndication. I sincerely hope this book helps to illuminate the path toward your success.

Chapter 1 – The Startling Power of Syndication

Welcome to the wonderful world of syndication.

Whether you're a beginner, an experienced broadcaster, a Web expert, a writer, or a content creator of any kind, you will love discovering the power of mass distribution that is possible with media syndication. Your compelling content can move from a single point of distribution to a national or even worldwide platform, allowing you to inform, entertain, and influence millions. All while earning good money.

Fortunately, you don't have to spend years learning how to get syndicated. You'll find all the answers you need in this book. If you're in a hurry, you can go directly to the chapters you need and get to work. But the more you can learn about all aspects of syndication, the better you will understand the total process. So I encourage you to read the entire book to absorb every detail that may be relevant to your project, or at least skim every chapter for helpful hints.

This book presents practical, how-to information on all major forms of media syndication: radio, television, print, and the Internet. Each medium has its own chapter; other chapters explore the broader topics of syndication. You will notice that various terms are used to describe what you are syndicating: *content*, *product*, *show*, and *program*. Just understand that all these terms refer to whatever it is you are planning to distribute to a mass audience via syndication.

Questions and Answers

As we begin, you probably have many questions. Let's tackle three very common questions about syndication right now.

Q: Is syndication a fast and easy process? How long does it take?

A: In most cases, it takes persistence, dedication, and a good deal of effort to succeed in syndication. But isn't that true of most worthwhile goals in life?

That being said, there are some 'syndication shortcuts' that can help to accelerate the process. We'll address them in this book. But you can expect that it will take at least several months before you start seeing progress.

Q: Is there any way to guarantee success in syndication?

A: There's no guarantee in syndication—just as there's no guarantee in any other business or personal venture. If anyone tells you they can guarantee you success in syndication, be very skeptical. But here's some good news: By following the proper steps and avoiding common pitfalls, you can vastly increase your odds of success.

Q: Is syndication an impossible goal for the average person?

A: Certainly not! In fact, it may be easier for the so-called average person to syndicate than it is for a highly intellectual individual. Brainy people may over-think the process and end up talking themselves out of it. Ordinary people are out there right now, steadily pursuing their syndication goals and achieving them.

Knowledge + Effort = Success

Let's consider that last question again: Is syndication an impossible goal for the average person? The question deserves a much fuller answer, because it goes to the heart of this book. If syndication success weren't possible for the average person, there'd be no point in writing several hundred pages on the topic. Obviously, we do believe it's possible, with the right knowledge and persistent effort. We are living proof of that.

Nevertheless, over the many years we've been in this business, we've found that most media people will tell you that syndication is extremely difficult.

"You have no concept how tough syndication is! There are so many roadblocks," they'll tell you. "It's virtually impossible to break in unless you have connections. You may lose your shirt! Don't even bother trying, because you're bound to fail."

Let's examine these negative statements in the cold light of day. Is the goal of success in syndication truly unreachable? Many other things in life are far more difficult than becoming syndicated, yet people somehow achieve those goals on a regular basis.

For example, we believe that becoming a medical doctor is much, much tougher than getting syndicated. To become a licensed physician requires four years of medical school—after four years of college. Your med school tuition will run about $100,000. After that, you'll spend three more years in residency. Then, and only then, will you be a doctor.

Many years ago, becoming an MD was my personal goal. I was a pre-med major at college and I stuck with it for several years. I watched surgeons perform operations, and I also talked with a number of doctors about my plans.

Not one of those physicians ever said to me, "You have no concept how hard it is. There are so many roadblocks, it's virtually impossible. Don't even bother trying because you'll fail." In fact, not a single one made discouraging comments of any kind! Instead, what I heard over and over again from them was the following advice:

- Read everything you can about the subject.
- Study and learn all the basics.
- Choose a specialty that interests you.
- Take advanced courses when you're ready.
- Find a good mentor.
- Follow the same steps that your mentor followed.

I have always considered physicians to be true professionals, if only because of this very helpful advice that several extremely busy medical men took the time to share with me years ago. (Note: This was NOT the advice I got from the "peanut gallery" of non-achievers.)

So why didn't I become an MD? That's easy. In my junior year of college I became completely, totally hooked on broadcasting. Suddenly, medicine didn't interest me in the least. But decades later when I syndicated my first radio show, I discovered that I had instinctively followed the same six steps to achieve that goal.

In fact, these steps can help you turn most any challenging dream you have into reality, whether it's learning to pilot a certain aircraft, building a profitable business, becoming a winning athlete in a particular sport, launching a worldwide charity, or becoming a success in media syndication.

Carefully review those six winning steps. You'll want to keep them in mind as we proceed.

Why Syndicate?

Why even attempt syndication? One quick answer: It can help you to make a difference in the world.

Today it's possible for anyone to leap from the crowd of unknown, voiceless people and step out onto the national stage. Once there, you can share your ideas and shape the views and opinions of millions of your fellow citizens. Or if you prefer, you can use the national platform to give others pure entertainment, or helpful advice and information.

How is it possible for just one person to achieve the far-reaching goal of connecting with millions? Through the startling power of syndication.

For the timid and meek, this may seem like a frightening concept. What crazy loophole in the system could possibly allow some nobody, especially one lacking elite credentials (such as an Ivy League education, blue-blood genetics, inherited wealth, or the proper set of opinions), to thrust him or herself into a position of influence and power?

Who Appointed Them?

In fact, some critics angrily point to individuals who seemingly have no right to such a powerful national platform. Depending on the crowd you hang with, you might hear names such as Rush Limbaugh, Ed Schultz, Sean Hannity, Howard Stern, Michael Savage, Chris Matthews, Bill Maher, Mark Levin, Randi Rhodes, Dr. James Dobson, Anne Coulter, or many others that some consider unwelcome media stars.

Some critical consumers have a hit parade of personalities whose politics are out of line with theirs, or whom they view as no-talent bums, or—the worst insult of all—boring beyond belief.

"Who appointed THEM to tell us what to think?"

Well, there's no conspiracy. The answer is: Nobody appointed them. In almost every one of these cases, these people made themselves national media figures—with maybe a little expert coaching and an assist from a network, syndication company, or agent.

They simply pursued their dreams of syndication. With talent, persistence, and hard work, they followed their chosen paths into radio, TV, newspapers, the Internet, or perhaps a combination of these media. And before you knew it, everyone was talking about them—fans and complainers alike.

Audiences Are Engaged

This brings up an interesting point about many of today's syndicated media personalities. Millions of people have opinions about them.

Today's audiences are engaged and involved, and they relate more than ever before to the personalities that they see on TV, hear on radio, and read online or in print publications.

He's OPPOSED TO ALL FORMS OF SILENCE

Whether the syndicators themselves are left, right, straight down the middle, religious or sacrilegious, angry or joyful, critical or approving, highbrow or down-to-earth, puritanical or hedonistic, entertaining or tedious—there's one thing they have in common. Their voices, images, and words have the power to capture the attention of the nation. Sometimes syndication audiences grow to massive numbers of deeply loyal fans.

There's room for all points of view and styles of presentation, because nearly all Americans (and, encouragingly, many people in other parts of the globe) believe in the free exchange of ideas. Those who cherish this freedom know that open dialogue, in which all voices speak freely, helps make this a better world for everyone.

Countering the Mass Media

Today, many Americans have become distrustful of the media and journalism in general. Large numbers of citizens believe they're being misinformed by broadcast networks, newspapers, or other media. They may also feel that bias pervades the supposedly factual news and information delivered by mainstream outlets. And they may wonder what they could possibly do to counter the spin they perceive in the media.

Of course, they could write a letter to the editor, which will get them some attention. They could pen an op-ed piece and hope it gets published. A column would give them slightly more exposure. They could go online and write a blog or create a podcast, and pray it gets noticed in an ever-growing ocean of online voices.

But none of these limited approaches can match the powerful impact of syndication.

When you host a nationally syndicated radio or TV show, write a nationally syndicated column, or make your content available in literally hundreds of places online via Internet syndication, your voice and your point of view have the potential to reach wide segments of the nation's population and make a significant impact. Whatever your ideas, beliefs, and opinions, as long as you're passionate about the content you create, there's a good chance that an audience out there is interested in what you can give them.

So the question to ask yourself is a simple one. Are you willing to give syndication a try?

In the pages ahead, we'll explore the risks and rewards. We'll share details of the various paths of syndication. Then you can decide for yourself if syndication is right for you.

The People Are There

Every day, lots of people are focused on the media. The power of all those people listening to you, watching you, or reading your words can be immense. They may be moved to buy the products and services you recommend, or moved to think deeply about what you say (and if you make a convincing argument, perhaps millions will begin to see things just as you do). There's always an audience for stimulating talk, opinions, and ideas about the events shaping today's world.

If entertaining and enlightening others is your style, we're guessing you may have already had a taste of this on a smaller scale. Perhaps you already host a local radio show or podcast, or you write a blog or local column.

If a certain musical genre or style strongly appeals to you, that might be your path to radio syndication. If you have an idea for a clever new TV show, that might be your doorway to national fame.

Or perhaps you're an author, public speaker, business owner, or expert in a certain field such as health, law, or finance. You might be a sports fan, or have a strong interest in a topic such as parenting, women's issues, the Internet, food and wine, minority matters, self-motivation, marketing, romance, pets, Hollywood gossip...you name it.

Your goal is to reach a wider audience, and syndication can make it happen for you.

Success in syndication does not require wealth (see the section in Chapter 2, 'Starting on a Shoestring in a Second Bedroom'). More important than money is persistence. You must keep the vision of what you want to achieve always in mind, until it becomes reality.

Smiles and High Fives

What does it feel like to make it in syndication? We invite you to imagine that right now. Picture the following scenes in your mind's eye. What would each of these life moments feel like to you?

- You are recognized at public gatherings as a top opinion leader.
- Profitable business deals come your way with far less effort.
- You notice you get much more respect from business associates.
- Your spouse and family brag about you to others they meet.
- People keep asking when you are going to write a book.
- You can't wait to get up and go to work every morning.
- Your kids suddenly think you're cool—and so do their friends.
- You are acknowledged publicly as a media personality.
- You get high fives from your friends and neighbors.
- Journalists call to ask for quotes for their news stories.
- Your opinions carry far more weight than ever before.
- You get many invitations to fun and interesting events.
- You overhear strangers dropping your name.
- People at your house of worship express quiet admiration.
- Emails arrive daily from fans across the country.
- Your personal "clout" factor grows in unimagined ways.
- You find yourself interviewing really famous people.
- You are approached by major media outlets for tie-ins.
- People get flustered when meeting you for the first time.
- You say your name, and someone says "Not THE (name)?"

By now, you may be wondering something. Along with influence, income, and an improved lifestyle, can syndication also provide love, respect, power, fame, and that indefinable "cool" factor that everyone dreams of having?

That's hard to say. But ponder this: Every one of the scenes above was described to us by people whose content had become nationally syndicated. If those great things happened for them, why not for you?

The Power of the Towers

Let's say you do a local radio show or even a podcast. You believe your show or podcast is good—in fact, you put a lot of thought and dedication into creating it. But until you syndicate it, you won't begin to understand the Power of the Towers—the magic effect of broadcast syndication.

It's what causes your show to transcend local, limited, narrow distribution. Broadcast syndication gives you blanket coverage of a region, or coast-to-coast coverage of the entire nation.

Try to imagine your voice, your ideas, your enthusiasm, and your passion being transmitted over the air by dozens or even hundreds of broadcast towers spanning the nation. When this happens, countless numbers of people can be moved by you, entertained by you, and informed by you. The result is, they respond to you. At the same time, advertisers will likely be willing to partner with you, so their message can reach your growing audience.

Old School and Still Growing

Let's face it: Traditional broadcast media is sometimes considered "old school" in today's digital world. But it remains an incredibly powerful force. A New York ad agency leader recently stated that advertisers vote with their pocketbooks, and they keep putting their dollars into "old media" for two reasons. First, many consumers trust it, and second, it is still the best way to reach a mass audience.

That's why radio and TV continue to have banner years in advertising revenue. Consumers seem to agree. For example, radio listening is still growing in this second decade of the 21st century. As of this writing, over-the-air radio has risen to a weekly audience of 242 million Americans, or about 93% of the population.

Media Dominates Discussions

Some everyday conversational catchphrases have become so familiar that most of us don't even notice them.

Sit quietly in a restaurant or other public place for a few minutes and listen to others talking. Before long, you'll hear somebody use a phrase like one of these:

- "I was listening to the radio this morning, and they said..."
- "Did you watch (TV show) last night? Wasn't it great?"
- "I caught something on the car radio today..."
- "Have you seen that new show about (topic)...?"
- "Couldn't believe what I heard (media personality) say today..."
- "I just read a great column I have to send you..."

As much as some like to denigrate the media, it relentlessly dominates our discussions—and often our points of view. The media makes a vast, ongoing contribution to the national dialogue. It also provides countless hours of entertainment and information to millions of people.

Hush Up, Kids!

When you were growing up, did you ever find yourself being shushed by a parent who wanted to hear something important on radio or TV?

"SSHHH, be quiet now!" they admonished you. "We've got to hear this!"

It's undeniable. What the media says at any given moment can be far more compelling than what our closest family members say.

It's an old joke in certain media circles. Supposedly, everyone who chooses a career in media was once shushed by their parents, who made it clear that the radio or TV was more important than they were! The thinking goes that a career in media was the kid's way of overcoming that early rejection. Who knows—there may be some truth to this psychology.

If syndication is your dream goal, heed this lesson well. The Hush Up, Kids factor is not one to be taken lightly. As a syndicated content creator, you'll serve your audience best by fully engaging your brain before you communicate. You'll survive by understanding the rules of libel and slander. And you should never forget that out there, somewhere, somebody is truly hanging on every word you say.

Trusted Personalities

When people are surveyed about how much they trust the media, the numbers are far from impressive. In fact, compared to past decades, trust in the media appears to be at an all-time low. These surveys are often worded in such a general way that people have nothing specific to focus on—"the media" is a faceless, generic concept.

But when surveys are taken regarding individual media personalities, it can be a completely different ballgame. The late Paul Harvey, for example, scored high on the trust factor with his millions of radio listeners. Approach the fans of a particular syndicated star, and you'll usually find that the star's favorability ratings are off the chart.

In syndication, it's possible to form a bond with listeners, viewers, or readers by letting them get acquainted with the "real you." This can help them feel like you're an old friend—even though they've never met you, and possibly never will. Be consistent in your style, your stated beliefs, and your way of doing things, and you'll soon start earning a mantle of trust.

As a syndicated personality, you can transcend the negative umbrella "media" label by being genuine and real with your audience. Over time, they will put their trust in you, and the bond can become very strong.

Suddenly, You're Everywhere

The Power of the Towers can put you into virtually every nook and cranny of this great nation. People will take you with them in the car while doing errands. Truckers will follow your words as they cruise the interstate. Weekend warriors will listen on headphones while exercising or doing chores. Office workers in their cubicles will tune in online. If you choose to syndicate to TV, viewers may tune you in just about anywhere, since television screens are ubiquitous these days. The same goes for Web syndication, with desktops, laptops, or mobile browsers always within reach.

Media is pervasive in America. Radios are found in most cars, as well as in 98% of homes. Many radio stations also stream their content online. The vast majority of homes have TV sets. Cable TV reaches 60% of the population. Many homes have TVs in the living room, kitchen, and bedroom. When you are syndicated, you become a part of the nation's hardwired, all-encompassing communications grid. There's really no imagining how many places you might turn up.

Online Is Big Time

According to Internet World Stats, as of this writing some 274 million Americans, or nearly 80% of the U.S. population, use the Internet.

Dig deeper and the statistics are even more staggering. The following numbers will undoubtedly be outdated by the time you read this book. Just consider them a snapshot of a constantly moving timeline. (Statistics are drawn from various credible sources, with thanks to www.royal.pingdom.com.)

Email

- 144 billion – Number of emails sent per day in 2012
- 294 billion – Average number of emails per day
- 2.2 billion – Number of email users worldwide
- 480 million – New email users since the year before

Websites

- 634 million – Number of websites as of December 2012
- 51 million – New websites in 2012

Domain names

- 100 million – .COM domain names at end of 2012
- 14.1 million – .NET domain names at end of 2012
- 9.7 million – .ORG domain names at end of 2012
- $2.4 million – costliest domain of 2012 (investing.com)

Internet users

- 2.4 billion – Internet users worldwide, mid-2012
- 14% – Increase in Internet users over the previous year
- 1.1 billion – Internet users in Asia
- 519 million – Internet users in Europe
- 274 million – Internet users in North America

Social media

- 187 million – Number of daily tweets in 2012
- 187 million – People on LinkedIn in 2012
- 200 million – Active people on Twitter as of 2012
- 1 billion – People on Facebook in 2012

Videos

- 14 million – Number of Vimeo users in 2012

- 35 Hours - Video content uploaded every minute to YouTube
- 4 billion – Videos watched per month on Facebook
- 182 million – Viewers of online video in US in 2012

Images

- 5 billion – Photos uploaded to Instagram in 2012
- 7 petabytes – Photos added monthly to Facebook
- 300 million – Photos added daily to Facebook

The massive growth of the Web means good things for syndication. Internet content syndication, full content syndication, opt-in syndication, and viral syndication are just some of the powerful ways to harness the power of the net to achieve a major impact. These Web tactics, and others, are worth considering. We'll cover them all in the pages ahead.

What the Internet offers in spades is amazing speed, as well as the potential for national and worldwide recognition by a vast audience. But successful Internet syndication may in some ways be more challenging than traditional media syndication. This is because there are so many competing messages clamoring for Web users' attention. To make your online syndication efforts really pay off, you must apply proven methods to cut through the clutter and rise above the noise.

Mobile Extends Web Content

Perhaps even more dramatic than Internet growth is the ongoing explosion in mobile phone use. According to Sybase, 70% of the world's population now has a mobile phone. That's over 5 billion mobile subscribers around the globe.

What about mobile use in the U.S.? An astonishing 9 in 10 Americans now have mobile phones. It's safe to predict that this 90% figure will climb even higher in the years ahead.

For a quick glimpse at where the next generation of Americans is headed, consider the fact that 85% of young people now have a mobile phone. For many of them, the Web is not something to be accessed from a desktop or laptop. Instead, it's as close and immediate as a smartphone.

Helping fuel the move to mobile is the ubiquitous Apple iPhone, which has surpassed several hundred million units sold. Meanwhile, competing mobile platforms are showing remarkable growth.

Smartphones extend the Internet to mobile use. A vast number of applications offer a dizzying array of options for consumers. Of particular interest are the apps that make it possible to consume media of all kinds, including traditional media, while on the go.

The Impact of Print

Believe it or not, newspapers remain influential in our world. Despite being tagged as "dinosaurs" in the present digital media environment, the print medium continues to fight a valiant battle against declining circulation numbers.

Many newspapers have extended their brands and content to the Web, which has added to their readership. Now local newspapers can easily reach national and global readers, at little additional cost. However, most papers have had little success monetizing their Web presence. Many struggle to find significant online revenues from advertising, online subscriptions, pay walls, or other means.

While the long-term business model of newspapers may appear discouraging, make no mistake. Newspaper content remains influential. In particular, large metropolitan dailies will likely continue making a strong impact for years to come, while retaining the cachet of true media clout.

If your goal is to write a daily or weekly syndicated newspaper column, or to draw a popular syndicated cartoon or comic strip, it is still possible to do so. You must understand that shrinking page counts and tight economics at newspapers make this a very challenging goal. But we'll share what we consider the best tactics for breaking into this business, if this is your dream. It may be worth pursuing as part of a multimedia syndication strategy. Once you have an established foothold in electronic media, it can help open the door to print syndication.

Still Skeptical?

As you have read, there are multiple paths for syndication: radio, television, Web, and print. For any one of these paths, the audience demand is there for fresh, quality content of all varieties.

Some of you may still be convinced that traditional media syndication remains an out-of-reach dream for the everyday person. The doubters might point to recent trends—for example, corporate consolidation in the broadcasting industry—as signs that it's now harder than ever to syndicate a show.

At our own company which specializes in syndication, we can tell you that this is definitely not the case. To cite the example above, radio stations owned by virtually every company in the business, including the corporate giants, happily carry the syndicated content our company offers. It's extremely rare to hear of a corporate edict that tells station managers they cannot accept independent syndication. If and when such a command comes down from above, it's almost always temporary in nature.

The fact is, stations want and need quality syndicated content more than ever before. With tight programming budgets, syndication helps stations broadcast the content they can't produce on their own. This in turn helps stations sell more commercials and boost their bottom line.

Doubters vs. Action Takers

It's easy for the doubters to sit on the sidelines and tell others about the risks of syndication. Fear of failure is probably at work here. The doubters feel it's best not to even try, because there's always a chance it won't work out.

Meanwhile, the positive action takers take a methodical approach to their goal. First, they learn all they can from books and other resources. They choose a particular niche as their specialty. Then, they formulate a plan and get advanced information or assistance. Many find a mentor, so they can mirror the steps the mentor followed on the road to success. In this way, their risk is minimized and their chances of success are maximized.

The preceding paragraph neatly sums up the best way to win the syndication game.

Before you turn the page to Chapter 2, candidly ask yourself how you approach each new day. Having a prosperity mindset, an optimistic attitude, and a determination to succeed are helpful factors in syndication. But along with the right mindset, it's important to learn the right steps in the process. It's our hope that this book will help you take the right steps, give you positive inspiration, and help you start moving toward the many rewards this wonderful business can provide.

Chapter 2 – A Syndication Story

It's time to share a story with you. Don't worry, this won't be a long boring tale—at least, it isn't meant to be!

What we will try to do here is briefly explain the steps we took to syndicate our own shows, and what motivated us to go for it. This is the first time we've ever gone into such detail about the background and the syndication process we followed. We're doing this with two goals in mind.

First, we're hoping you'll discover some helpful ideas from the steps we followed. We'll get into the specifics, simply because some insignificant point we make could strike a chord in you and inspire you to go for it, too.

Second, our story will give you a real-life, honest-to-goodness example of how somebody virtually unknown to the national audience (as we were) can end up hosting two syndicated shows heard on a total of 635 radio stations (which we now do).

Start at the Beginning

In the dog-eat-dog world of corporate radio, it has been quite a climb in the media food chain—and at a relatively young age. From a corner office in Manhattan, I was the manager of a corporate flagship radio station with a budget in the tens of millions and a veteran staff.

But we're getting ahead of things. Let's rewind to when I was still a young student attending Williams College. The course load was a grind. But one fateful evening, while exploring the campus, I stumbled upon the student-run radio station. WCFM was hidden away in the basement of the old student union.

The station lobby was rundown and well-worn, but it felt like entering the ultimate fun factory. That station had plenty of the two things I loved: music and electronics. Having grown up listening to radio, I'd often visited my hometown Top 40 station to request tunes from the local DJs, who appeared to be topping 40 themselves.

But watching kids my own age actually run a radio station suddenly made me realize I could do it, too.

Here's why we begin the story in those early radio days. That experience set a pattern, one that stayed true for decades to come. Honestly, I'm not the brightest bulb in the pack. But upon discovering how much fun radio could be, it was remarkably easy to become an overachiever, investing lots of time and effort. The volunteer student staff must have picked up on this, because they soon elected me station manager.

The station's signal covered the campus, but not far beyond it. And we had a non-commercial license. Despite these shortcomings, we somehow convinced the mighty ABC to make us a network affiliate. Undoubtedly, we were the tiniest in their chain. We also recruited lots of students to become DJs and fill the empty slots in our schedule. Thanks to their efforts, the station finally stayed on the air 7 days a week, 18 hours a day. We found funding for a much-needed station renovation, and built fancy new production studios. All of this progress took time and effort.

First Real Job

Then out of the blue, a commercial AM-FM station in a nearby town offered me a job as an announcer and news reader. It was a bit scary being on a "real" station, but after a few hours we felt right at home. The typical air shift ended at 1 a.m. Then we'd sign off the stations, shut down the transmitters, and lock up. Next was the drive back to the dorm on a deserted highway, a few hours of study, a bit of sleep, and then off to 8 a.m. classes.

It was a crazy schedule, but we were having a great time doing it. It's amazing how much energy you can generate on a diet of cold pizza and burgers, when you love what you're doing.

After graduating, we loaded up a U-Haul and headed to Chicago. We'd never been to that town before, but the Windy City truly had some remarkable radio stations.

Major Market Radio

Appropriately enough, we landed an internship position at WIND Radio with the title of Talk Show Producer. If college radio had been fun, major market radio was a blast. Time off meant little. Being a true geek, the ultimate goal was to be at the station whenever possible.

Chicago radio fans may recognize some of the legendary on-air talent we were fortunate enough to work with: Dave Baum, Ed Schwartz, Clark Weber, Joel Sebastian, Gary Gears, Connie Szerszen, Doug Dahlgren, Howard Miller, and others. Being around professionals like these was a great education.

During those years, we found time to study for and acquire an FCC first-class license. Fixing transmitters wasn't of interest, but a first-class ticket seemed like another key toward mastery of radio.

At one point at WIND, I worked 21 days straight, double shifts, without a day off. Obviously, the boss loved that, but strangely enough, so did I. While I'd never again devote that many nonstop hours to a job, I believe that early total commitment paid off much later. It was like a highly accelerated training course. As a talk show producer, we got to meet and chat with many fascinating people, including movie actors, recording artists, TV stars, and newspaper columnists.

The next job was at WBZ in Boston, as Production Director, but then a promotion came: Executive Producer in charge of talk shows. Still just a young guy, yet they asked me to be in charge of legendary radio figures that included Larry Glick, Dave Maynard, Carl de Suze, and others. As you might expect, they ended up teaching us plenty.

The Mighty 1190

WOWO Fort Wayne was the next assignment, as Program Director. Though Fort Wayne is not a major market, I consider the station a giant. This 50,000 watt music station had a very positive impact on me. Once again we got to work with true legends, including Bob Sievers, Jack Underwood, Chris Roberts, Ron Gregory, and others. Sievers had been the morning man for nearly 50 years, and he loved pointing out that I was young enough to be his grandson. Still, he was open to new ideas, as was everyone else there. A real team effort resulted in the station's achieving an amazing 25.0 Arbitron share, the highest overall rating of any music station in America at that time.

KDKA Pittsburgh then beckoned. There, the job was to manage both the programming and news departments. Again, there were many local radio superstars, including John Cigna, Fred Honsberger, Art Pallan, Mike Pintek, Bob Logue, and more. Thanks to their hard work, the ratings jumped by over 50 percent and we all had lots of fun.

Now the career began moving faster. Next came a return to Chicago as Director, News and Programming for all-news WBBM. What a top-notch news staff! But there was a threat—a new competitor, WMAQ. Strategic programming and marketing helped us block the challenge, and in the process our ratings grew sizably.

Not Quite a Dream

CBS was pleased, and the reward was a dream job: VP/General Manager. But the position was not in Chicago. The station they asked us to run was all-talk WCAU in Philadelphia. It was a good news/bad news deal. The good news was finally getting to manage a major market station. The bad news, it was the worst performing station in the company. While the ratings did rise substantially over the next 18 months, growth wasn't fast enough to make the bean counters happy.

Suddenly the brass decided a transfer to New York was in order. The struggling outlet in Philly was no longer our problem. Such is the volatile nature of the media business.

The Escape Hatch

For the next few years, my memorable job was VP/General Manager of WCBS New York. As the company's flagship all-news station, it was located in the company's Black Rock headquarters in midtown Manhattan. Managing this operation was quite a responsibility. It was sometimes exciting, especially during breaking news stories (such as the Persian Gulf War). At those times, the news team went into high gear. The staff was extremely professional, and overall, it was an enjoyable time.

But unfortunately, corporate politics factor into most corporate settings, and this was no exception. There were more than a few personal fiefdoms to overcome. And some there didn't seem to grasp what we were trying to do with the station. Overall, the work was becoming a grind.

It felt as though we'd been on a long train ride through fascinating lands. But we'd gotten so caught up in the journey that we missed the spot where we should have disembarked. Now the question was, what to do about it.

No Guts, No Glory

Looking back, it's clear that challenging times can bring about the best opportunities.

Having climbed the company ladder, it was time to leave it—but for what? The answer wasn't quite clear, but the expression, "No Guts, No Glory" certainly applied. Risk and reward go hand in hand. Now was the time to go for it.

There were long conversations with various mentors, a number of whom ran their own companies. This convinced me I should do the same. The nation was in the midst of a recession, but the research showed that bad economic times can actually be the right time to start a new business. People are more willing to negotiate and more open to working with new partners in bad times than they are when things are booming.

Sure enough, new clients showed up quickly. Some of them were stations we'd previously managed. Others were former competitors, such as WMAQ. It's surprising how new opportunities can appear when you move forward with confidence.

By now you may be wondering what this story has to do with syndication.

"The Success Journal"

By this point in the career, we'd accumulated a good deal of knowledge and experience. That know-how included how to program a radio station, manage a station, negotiate contracts, sell advertising—you name it. We'd worked in small-market, medium-market, and major-market radio. Now we had a successful radio consulting business.

Despite all this, you may be surprised to learn that I knew very little about radio syndication. Other than signing syndication deals on behalf of my stations, I didn't really understand the intricacies of the business.

But while working with WMAQ, we had the opportunity to create a little business show. Each short episode told a little-known story behind a successful product or brand name. On a whim, the decision was made to name this new feature *The Success Journal*. Perhaps, it was a way for us to recapture some of the fun of those early on-air experiences in radio.

Three samples were produced, and played for the station's General Manager. After a long pause, she slowly said that it wasn't a bad show. She was even kind enough to agree to put it on the air—at 4 a.m. Sunday morning! People laugh when they hear this story, but it's true.

Even though it seemed like a trivial thing, we put all we could into writing and voicing that show. For some reason, the stories of people who turned nothing into something resonated inside and struck an emotional chord. Maybe it was because I was unconsciously doing the very same thing. Truly, there was no clue at this point how big this little show would soon become.

Looking back, it's clear what made the show click. It wasn't my voice, which isn't so great. Nor was it how the show was produced. What gave it sparks was our fascination with entrepreneurial achievement. The passion and enthusiasm for these stories came through the radio and connected with listeners, as the following story reveals.

A Surprise Endorsement

One day, the station held a listener input session. This was what researchers call a Focus Group. A group of station listeners was brought in, given punch and cookies, and seated around a big table. A moderator began asking them what they liked or disliked about the station.

I was sitting at the table along with the station GM. None of the panel members had a clue as to my identity. I might have been another listener, for all they knew.

One unforgettable dark-haired little old lady was seated at the table. Out of the blue she piped up, "Ya know, there's a short program that comes on very early Sunday mornings. I just love that thing! I listen for it every Sunday. It's about successful people. I tell you, it's fantastic!"

The GM kicked my shin under the table, and I was barely able to avoid reacting.

Early the next morning, the GM called and asked, "Was that your Mom?" We both laughed. Then she said, "Hey, how about we put *The Success Journal* on every afternoon?"

Now I had to write five stories a week, which meant five times the work. But it was fun to see my show expand. Being on weekdays meant thousands more people were hearing my show. I began to get positive feedback. People started asking me what this signified. Was I looking to expand my show further, or perhaps change my career?

That sparked a life-changing idea. Why not try syndicating this little show?

The Impossible Dream

It seemed like an impossibility. As I've mentioned, I was fairly clueless about the syndication process, although I'd negotiated quite a few syndication deals in my career. I knew that stations were always looking for interesting, different, informative, and entertaining programs. But that was a far cry from understanding all the ins, outs, and nuances of how to successfully syndicate a radio program.

That's when I began to immerse myself in learning all I could about syndication. Back then, there were no books on the topic. Nor were there any information products. The Internet was just getting started. I tried phoning some syndicators, but all of them were very close-lipped about the process. And some of them simply slammed down the phone when I told them why I was calling.

But slowly, by persistent digging, the picture gradually started to come into focus.

Being in Chicago, it wasn't hard to find industry insiders who were willing to let me buy them lunch or a drink. One lunch tab might pay off with one new piece of useful information, or the name of a vital contact. After a couple of months of this informal research, I was starting to get the lay of the land.

Leap of Faith

One day we simply decided to make the jump into syndication.

In fact, there's really no other way to do it, starting out. You just have to have faith in the outcome. Learn all you can, study and absorb the process, as you're doing here. But don't over-think it. Otherwise, your brain will find some loose thread of doubt, and your dream will start to unravel. And you'll talk yourself right out of it.

In fact, we've seen this happen any number of times with show hosts, despite their having a product that could be very popular. They let the fear factor overtake them. And they soon go back to their mundane routine.

But if you've read this far, we're guessing you might have the same dream. So here's some advice for you: When you feel the time is right, don't hesitate. Make the leap. Go for it and trust your instincts that it will work. Everyone has to do this at some point to achieve something truly meaningful.

Starting on a Shoestring Budget

In our case, a second bedroom became ground zero for *The Success Journal*. First came a makeshift desk made of a sheet of plywood to save money, followed by working on the project every spare hour possible. It was at that desk that the first marketing materials were created (much of it guesswork), along with production of a rough audio demo, which would later be revised several times. With the demo and marketing kit, the next step was to contact radio stations across the country. Although there was a good deal of rejection, it was an exciting time. It seemed like something big was right around the corner.

You might think that the stations where we'd once worked would be the first to welcome the new show. Only one of them did: the small town AM-FM station where I'd landed my first real job, while in college. They were happy to carry it, for which I will always be grateful.

Honestly, it was not bothersome to have others reject me, because there are some 10,000 stations in the U.S. It seemed certain that more stations would soon be adding the show. Imagine how exciting it was, at the end of the first full month, to have signed up 15 stations!

Looking Like a Winner

Around that time, we bumped into an old friend on the street, and began telling her about the new syndicated show. Then we excitedly said, "And it's already on 15 stations!"

She replied, "Wow! Did you say 115 stations?"

"No," we replied. "FIFTEEN stations."

"Ohhh," she said, with obvious disappointment in her voice.

If you decide to syndicate, you can expect a few humbling reactions like this. Even your closest friends may dismiss your initial enthusiasm. What may seem big and exciting to you might seem like small potatoes to them. This is probably because they've been exposed to media hype about shows being on hundreds of stations, columnists appearing in hundreds of papers, and so on. So your early, small handful of outlets may appear lame to them.

Just realize that everybody, including you, has to start somewhere. If you stick with it, if you have compelling content, and if you follow the right steps, chances are you'll eventually have some impressive numbers to share with others.

Charting My Growth

Along the way, we tried many different syndication strategies. Some worked, but many did not. We refused to let anything slow down the effort. We just kept pushing forward. The station list kept growing, and the handmade chart posted on the wall of the second bedroom reflected the upward trend.

When we reached 35 stations, it felt like a major milestone. We began making money from the show about then. And the income was a big help in paying the bills.

At this point, I was still holding down the consulting job with individual stations. (If you have an income-producing job, I suggest you hang onto it as long as possible—at least until your syndication project starts earning real money.)

A Fateful Friday

What led to the final leap to total freedom happened on a beautiful summer afternoon. It was the Friday of Labor Day weekend.

We'd gotten a call from a manager at WMAQ. They wanted to hold a budget meeting—at 5:30 p.m. that afternoon. So there we sat, several hours later, trapped in a conference room at Chicago's NBC Tower. We all listened as the budget numbers were being recited. My eyes were drawn to the large window.

Down below on Lake Michigan, there were dozens of sleek sailboats bobbing up and down in the blue water. People were out there having a good time, free to enjoy the glorious weather. And here we all were, cooped up in a stuffy conference room for no apparent reason, other than to hear a turgid discussion of budget numbers.

Silently, I told myself it was high time to escape the corporate world and experience the freedom to set schedules and plan for the future. In making this bold choice, we were trusting in syndication to carry things forward.

Riding a Rocket

It was a leap of faith, but the belief was there. With fulltime devotion to the project, it would be a success.

Mind you, we didn't just sit back after that and hope for the best. Nor did we start sleeping until noon every day. We actively worked at promoting and growing the show, day after day, just like a full-time job. But it didn't feel like work, because all efforts were going toward personal independence and the ideal kind of lifestyle for myself and my family.

Having that enthusiasm helped to recruit others to help the effort. There were more secrets of syndication to learn and apply. And before long, the show was on 50 stations, then 75 stations, 100 stations, 150 stations.

By then, *The Success Journal* was not only paying the bills, but it was earning a good income.

Just to bring this story right up to the present, we will quickly share what's happened since that time.

The Rest of the Story

With *The Success Journal* in so many markets, people began asking us for assistance.

There was an obvious opportunity to provide others with syndication services. Our company, Syndication Networks, has assisted a vast array of clients, large and small, with their syndication plans. Our clients range from major networks, to veteran broadcasters, to individuals getting into syndication for the first time.

A few years ago, there was the time and interest to host a second show: *InfoTrak*, a weekly interview program. Today it's on 576 stations, and still growing. *The Success Journal* is still going strong, too. Hard to believe that it's now approaching 20 years on the air.

Some years ago, our company entered the Internet radio sector in a big way with the launch of TalkZone.com. The site contains many thousands of hours of talk shows, created by an ever-growing roster of talented show hosts. We stream this high-quality audio and video content 24/7 to a national and worldwide audience.

What Can You Learn from All This?

Here are the key take-away points from this chapter.

First, no matter how experienced you are, or how much you think you know, nothing major will happen for you until you make the deliberate choice to break out of your comfort zone. Just four examples of my leaps of faith:

- When we accepted the first job at a "real" radio station
- When we traveled to Chicago for the first major market job
- When we quit the New York radio position
- And when making the jump to full-time syndication

Each time we took a plunge into the unknown, the risk paid off. Let's face it: If things hadn't worked out, it wouldn't have been the end of the world. Life would have gone on. But my philosophy is that you'll never know what you missed if you never try anything new!

The second point to take away is this: No matter how much you already know about radio, TV, newspapers or the Internet, you probably don't know enough about syndication. That was definitely true in my case. Today, there's much more information floating around than there was back then. But unfortunately, a good deal of that info is distorted or incomplete.

Third, it's important to have faith in the process to make it happen for you. That's true whether your goal is syndication success in radio, TV, newspapers, or the Web.

IF

you have good syndicated content, namely something of compelling quality to entertain others and attract an audience...

AND

you follow the right steps to market your content to the proper media outlets...

AND

you remain persistent, focused, positive, and determined...

THEN

success will eventually unfold, your content will be syndicated, and you will enjoy the rewards this business can give you: freedom, recognition, income, a better lifestyle, and more.

After many years in syndication, we firmly believe that this is the simple and proven formula that can deliver results.

Chapter 3 – Sizing Up Syndication

After reading my story, you may be wondering whether syndication can be part of your future, too. This chapter can help you decide if this is a goal worth pursuing.

Begin by considering which medium might best suit you as a syndication launch pad. Every popular medium for syndication has strengths and weaknesses to weigh. There are also differing challenges and hurdles for first-time syndicated content creators.

Hearing, Seeing, Reading

One undeniable fact is that different people gather information in different ways.

Depending on your overall goals in pursuing syndication, you might wish to consider what type of audience you wish to attract. There are subtle and not-so-subtle differences among the typical consumers of one medium over another.

Canadian philosopher Marshall McLuhan once broke down different forms of media into what he called "cool" and "hot" categories. He considered radio a hot medium, because it demands attention and participation from the listener. Radio has no visual component, yet humans are visual creatures. So it's natural for most listeners to create their own mental pictures while listening to the radio, which means there's greater mental involvement.

A cool medium, on the other hand, is one that requires less involvement, because it provides plenty of sense stimuli. An example McLuhan gave of a cool medium is television. You may have noticed that it's easy to disengage the mind while watching TV, because the tube provides both pictures and sound. There's lots of sensory stimulation, so less mental participation is required.

Whether or not you buy into McLuhan's concepts, they're useful for describing the different ways in which audiences relate to radio, TV, newspapers, and the Web.

Radio Days

Decades ago, radio was king. It was America's primary broadcast medium from the 1920s to the 1950s. Old-time radio shows of that era were highly popular. These stories featured mysteries, dramas, and comedy, with live actors and music. Listeners often became intensely engaged with these shows.

"Hey - 104.5? Your kid's temperature happens to be my favorite radio station!"

In the 1960s, social experts noted that people could clearly recall the details of the old-time radio shows, decades after they had been broadcast. Yet these same interviewees were barely able to remember similar details of TV shows they had recently viewed.

Why was this the case? No doubt it was because of the higher level of mental involvement that radio requires, compared to television. The mind-pictures we create for ourselves can be powerful and memorable. Comedian and broadcaster Stan Freberg once stated his belief that radio stretches the imagination. When asked if TV also stretches the imagination, Freberg replied, "Yes, but only up to 21 inches."

Making a Connection

Radio is a portable medium that naturally lends itself to syndicated hosts who have an engaging, friendly, and lively style. Because of its participatory nature, radio is also a medium that can form a personal, one-on-one connection with the listener. You might even hear listeners describe the medium as their "companion" or "friend."

Talented radio hosts understand the intimate nature of radio. They use it to their advantage by emphasizing a personal, friendly, and direct style—just as one might speak when conversing privately with a close, trusted friend. The result is that listeners start to feel a kinship with the host, as they might with a family member, even though they may have never met the host or even seen his or her face.

Consumers who enjoy radio also appreciate its on-the-go nature. Radio can entertain and inform users at the office, in the car, at the gym, and during other daily activities.

Radio also pairs well with other media. According to research, it's not uncommon for some media-hungry consumers to "double up" or even "triple up" by combining radio listening with Web surfing and/or reading print media.

Selling anything on the radio usually requires repeating a consistent message over time. If you were asked to recall some radio advertising that you've heard, you'd probably mention a message that aired again and again. A familiar sales message, phone number musical jingle, clever mnemonic, or snappy slogan is rarely forgotten by the audience—even years later—once it becomes implanted in their mind through repeated airings.

TV—It's Not Just "Radio with Pictures"

Turning again to McLuhan's terminology, let's consider television. As we've explained, TV is a cool medium because its nature is less participatory than radio's, while providing the user with lots of sensory stimuli.

You'll rarely hear anyone say, "Last night I zoned out in front of the radio for hours!" On the other hand, television has the power to induce near trance-like consumption in some viewers.

This is not to say that most television viewers are undiscriminating or unable to think for themselves. Just the opposite is usually the case. However, a well-produced TV program definitely can command and capture an audience's attention in a way no other medium can.

Network television is probably the last truly mass medium in America, with events such as the Super Bowl pulling in over 100 million viewers. No other medium to date can induce so many users to consume identical content simultaneously.

Rapid-Fire Images

TV delivers a steady stream of rapid-fire images and sounds. This content flow fills in all the blanks for the user, leaving little to the imagination. All the medium asks of the viewer is to sit back, watch, and absorb. The fast flow of pictures and sounds provides uninterrupted continuity in the messages being delivered.

Some social scientists theorize that humans have an inbuilt ability to stare at a flickering television screen for many hours at a time.

One reason, they say, may be that it represents the modern equivalent of the proverbial campfire or hearth.

For many centuries before the video age, countless generations spent every evening of their lives sitting and staring into a flickering fire. Perhaps you've found yourself doing this at home with your fireplace, or outdoors at a campfire.

Aside from exchanging fire and smoke for an electronic screen, there's another big difference between the fireplace and TV. Back in the day, people conversed with each other during those family fireside hours. These were the hours when they shared information and personal stories. Now, for the most part, TV does all the informing and storytelling, while viewers sit in silence.

How captivating is the boob tube? Well, here's just one example: Diet doctors caution against eating snacks during tube time, because TV can thoroughly rivet one's attention. The danger is that you will consume vast amounts of calories without even realizing it. Some medical experts consider TV a factor in the nation's obesity epidemic.

Millions of consumers enjoy nothing better than sitting down to watch a TV show without interruption or distraction. Many consider it their reward at the end of a long day. When other commitments arise during their regular TV time, technology comes to the rescue. VCRs and DVRs have made it easy to time-shift content. Viewers can choose when they want to watch their favorite programs.

Quick Cuts and Eye Candy

Modern production techniques have made TV broadcasts easy to watch and, for the most part, seamless to the eye. When something important appears onscreen, the camera zooms in to give us a clearer image. Televised sports events use cutaways and instant replays to show every possible angle of the game. When there's a lull in the action, the director can maintain the rapid pace of the broadcast by inserting stored video clips or images. We've all grown accustomed to quick cuts and lots of eye candy to keep our attention riveted to the screen, no matter what the content.

A talented TV producer with a reasonable budget can combine attractive set design, good lighting, clever graphics, and a solid script to create a program with lots of visual appeal and entertainment value. Such a program can literally captivate a viewing audience.

Television's ability to create attractive pictures makes it a powerful selling medium. Viewers can see an idealized vision of a product or service and the "proof is in the pictures," convincing them to buy.

Sales Power

In the case of direct-response TV ads and infomercials, advertisers have to do more than make the products look good. They also have to snap viewers out of the passive viewing state and motivate them to place an order right away. Hence the familiar phrase, "Order before midnight tonight!" and other such calls to action.

Although much of our media experience has been in radio, I got an early lesson in the power of TV. One evening I appeared in a brief interview clip on a Chicago TV station. My image was probably onscreen for a total of five to seven seconds. The next day, walking down a busy Chicago street, two different people stopped me within the span of a few minutes. Each of the strangers asked my name, adding, "I saw you on TV last night!" I thought to myself, "Good thing you didn't blink or you would have missed me!"

Visual Recognition

With this story in mind, just imagine how powerful the recognition factor might be for a full-time syndicated TV personality. A high level of visual recognition can literally throw open doors, while providing lasting credibility and impact. On the other hand, high recognition can also become a burden over the long term. Those who might find it a burden would be better off choosing syndication in a medium with less direct visibility.

There are pluses and minuses to both approaches. Either way, the personal recognition factor is something to keep in mind when it comes to television.

Television Syndication

While we're on the topic of TV, let's delve into a few points about television syndication.

Most readers understand the concept of a television network, and are very familiar with the "big four" U.S. TV networks: CBS, NBC, ABC, and Fox. Each of these big companies is, at its heart, a content and ad sales factory.

A TV network buys original programs from third-party producers, and it may also produce some of its own programming, such as news and sports content. The network schedules this content to air within specified network time blocks on an established network of affiliated broadcast TV stations. The network also sells the national commercial slots within these programs to national advertisers.

The Local Station

Local TV affiliates benefit from this relationship because they are given local spots within the network content. So a limited number of "avails" are designated for the local stations, who sell them to local advertisers.

Hence that familiar phrase often heard on network TV: "We'll be back after these words from your local station." That's a sure sign you're about to view spots sold by the local outlet.

For a local TV station, there are other benefits to being a network affiliate. It can give an overall ratings lift to the station, thanks to the network viewership. It can lend prestige, and provide branding and marketing opportunities for the local station.

Outside the typical network time blocks, such as early morning and prime time, a local station must fill all of its remaining hours of airtime with non-network content. It may do this by airing some locally-produced shows, such as local news. It can air licensed content, such as movies from a film library. The station might also sell blocks of airtime, such as infomercials.

Most importantly for our discussion here, the local station can also air syndicated programs to fill its program schedule. We will discuss this in much greater depth in an upcoming chapter.

Whatever it broadcasts, the station hopes to sell that content to advertisers, one way or another. That's how a local station stays in business and earns a profit for its owner.

Off-Network Syndication

Once a TV network such as CBS, Fox, NBC, or ABC has aired its original, fresh content on its affiliated stations and reaped a big profit from ad sales, what happens to that content?

It often gets syndicated.

Assuming a network show pulled a reasonable viewing audience during its first run, that show may be made available to local stations as "off-network syndication."

In this way, the producer and/or network can reap significant, ongoing profits from the "used" content. Local stations will gladly pay for high-quality off-network syndication.

When you see a show such as "Seinfeld" on a local station, that's an example of off- network syndication. As co-producer and co-creator of that show, comedian Jerry Seinfeld has earned hundreds of millions from off-network syndication. In addition, he has benefited from robust DVD sales of the program.

Off-network syndication revenue, product sales, and other forms of show-related income are what I call "back-end profits," or BEP. Keep BEP in mind, because it will be your good friend no matter what form of syndication you choose to pursue. We'll be mentioning it in the pages ahead.

What's in It for the Local Station?

How does a local station benefit from airing an off-network syndicated show? Very simply, the station sells ads that run within that show for big dollars, even though it is a rerun. Fans tune in again and again to see a show they love. Some shows, such as "I Love Lucy" and "The Honeymooners," remain popular many decades after their original network run.

It is common for such syndicated TV shows to be slightly edited. This lets the local stations insert a few more minutes of commercials. This, in turn, makes it possible for the local stations to pay the syndicator even higher prices for the rights to air the show.

First-Run Syndication

Off-network is just one form of TV syndication. Independent producers also create first-run shows, and syndicate those shows directly to local stations. One highly successful example of this is "Star Trek: The Next Generation."

The original "Star Trek" series first aired on the NBC Television Network and later followed the path of off-network syndication. But Paramount chose to syndicate the "Next Generation" series directly to stations and avoided network distribution. In so doing, they took a risk that the show might not be accepted by stations. But the risk paid off handsomely. Paramount reaped all the rewards without having to share any lucrative first-run ad inventory with a TV network.

Paramount continues to enjoy massive BEP from the entire "Star Trek" franchise: ongoing syndication, DVD sales, cable TV distribution, licensing fees, motion pictures, books, apparel, and so on.

Other First-Run Shows

Other examples of first-run syndication include children's programming (such as cartoons), game shows, how-to shows, entertainment shows, dramas, reality shows, and talk shows. All these TV products and more have been successfully syndicated to local stations on a first-run basis. If you choose to syndicate to television, you will likely be wise to choose one of these proven categories for your show.

Producers create such shows and syndicate this content to stations. The stations air these first-run shows during their local programming hours. A show that has "legs" may develop into a valuable franchise that can give the syndicator an income stream lasting for years or even decades after the first run.

Public TV

Public TV has a system of syndication similar to the above, with a critical difference. Producers create and distribute their content only to non-commercial TV stations. Since public stations are not licensed to air commercials, there must be some other value exchanged for the program content. Funds for public TV's syndicated content typically come from corporate and viewer donations.

We will explore public radio and TV syndication in more detail in the pages ahead.

Radio Syndication

Modern radio syndication has one major difference from TV syndication, and a number of minor differences.

The major difference is this: In modern commercial radio, there are no networks that dominate the programming of local radio affiliates. For example, you won't hear multi-hour blocks of CBS radio shows on a CBS-affiliated radio station.

In the first half of the last century, when radio was the nation's dominant source of broadcast entertainment, the networks filled up many daily hours on their affiliated stations. In the mid-20th century, network radio's "prime time" was in the evening, much like TV today. Millions of families would gather around the glowing dial to hear their favorite network radio shows.

In the 1950s that entire structure went out the window, when radio stations were forced to compete with TV's rapid growth. Radio had to take a very different path to survive and thrive.

Modern-Day Radio

One obvious solution to the threat of TV was for local radio stations to produce live, local programming around the clock. This sparked the rise of the disc jockey and their spinning platters, on thousands of radio stations across the country.

By the late 50s, most families no longer had a big radio anchored in the living room, because a TV set had replaced it. So radio had to go near to where the listeners were: the car dashboard, the kitchen counter, the bedroom nightstand, the office desk, even the shirt pocket—in the form of a tiny transistor radio.

Content from big radio networks was also curtailed to hourly newscasts and other small chunks of station airtime, in exchange for a reduced amount of commercial inventory being given to the network.

And today there's virtually nothing that can be called off-network syndication in radio. Nearly all radio syndication consists of first-run content provided by independent producers, a variety of networks, and other providers.

Dozens of Radio Networks

Radio differs in another way from broadcast television. In the world of broadcast TV, relatively few networks dominate the industry. But in radio, there are dozens of networks all competing for airtime. Even corporate station owners with hundreds of stations in their portfolios must battle the independents, which provide some highly rated, well-niched products—products that many program directors are eager to carry.

Much syndicated talk and sports content is carried live by radio stations. In the case of talk shows, live carriage allows real-time listener participation and call-ins, as well as host commentary on breaking news.

Stations have the option to air this content live, inserting their local commercials on the fly. But a station can easily "tape delay" a live show for later playback, to fit their local schedule.

Few Radio Reruns

Sometimes a station will repeat a highly popular, previously-aired syndicated show at an off-peak time. But this is hardly as common in radio as it is in television. Radio reruns are a relative rarity.

Syndicated radio products that do not need to be live are generally produced in advance and fed to stations for later broadcast. Examples include music shows, short-feature vignettes, production libraries, public affairs shows, and how-to shows.

The steps to successful radio syndication are explored in a later chapter.

Syndication in Black and White

There are media consumers who naturally gravitate toward content they can read, re-read, and absorb. They find this content in daily and weekly newspapers and, of course, online.

For some consumers, the printed word is a more credible and trustworthy form of communication than other media. For example, if your name is on the byline of a newspaper column, you will be viewed by many readers as possessing a considerable degree of gravitas, even before they've read the first word in your column.

The aforementioned media philosopher Marshall McLuhan considered print a hot medium—meaning it invites the user's mental participation and requires plenty of involvement. In other words, you can't just stare glassy-eyed at a newspaper and get much out of it. Instead, you have to actively scan the pages, read the words, and think about them to absorb the content.

While newspaper readership is undeniably in decline, most of the print dailies and weeklies are taking steps to extend their platforms to the Web. This hasn't resolved their revenue issues, but it has certainly supplemented their total readership.

So if you are drawn to the idea of writing a column or creating a print cartoon, and you are able to break into this competitive field, it's a sure bet you will have regular readers, both in print and online.

For entry into the world of print syndication, the ability to write well is an obvious requirement. Indeed, anyone who wants to succeed as the creator of a syndicated column should have a genuine talent for turning a distinctive phrase.

Equally important is the ability to meet strict deadlines without fail, and to consistently deliver the goods. There's no "calling in sick" when you are a syndicated newspaper columnist. However, thanks to laptop computers, iPads, and other modern writing tools, it's possible to hammer out a finished product virtually anytime and anywhere, and instantly send it off for national distribution.

Underwear at the Kitchen Table

There is no doubt something very appealing to many creative folks about print syndication.

Imagine achieving national fame and influence, along with a very healthy income, simply by typing a certain number of words into your computer on a regular basis. You can even tap on that keyboard while in your underwear, sitting at the kitchen table.

Achieving such a career result may seem like an impressive and bold feat. But it is not impossible. Many well-known people have made it happen for themselves. And they weren't well-known until they became syndicated in print.

We'll cover the steps required to break into the competitive field of print syndication in a later chapter.

Weaving a Syndication Web

Let's now touch on Internet syndication. The Web is a step away from traditional media, and a different path from the old-line mass media of radio, TV, and newspapers.

While the Web is definitely a form of mass media, chances are your syndicated online content will end up reaching a more fragmented audience than it will in traditional media syndication. This is simply because of the numbers involved and the unique nature of the Web.

Unlike any form of traditional media, the Internet is a distribution platform that's wide open to all sorts of content (print, audio, video, still images, artwork, and more) created by millions upon millions of online participants.

By syndicating your Web content, you'll reach aggregated numbers of Web users. This will put you ahead of Web content creators who are not syndicated, and who distribute content to only a single online distribution point, such as via their own website.

However, no matter how hard you work at syndicating Web content, chances are it will not impact the many millions of consumers that it could with traditional radio, television, or print syndication.

This is not necessarily a bad thing. If your goal is to reach only a particular segment or niche of online users, Web syndication might be just what you're looking for.

What Online Syndication Means

There's another difference between old-fashioned media and the Web. In traditional media, the word *syndication* means just one thing: You feed your content, in its original form, to a number of distribution points. This enables you to reach a national audience and earn an income, at the same time.

On the Web, *syndication* may be used to describe a number of things. For example, there is Internet content syndication, which may comprise article writing, Internet radio and podcasts, and video distribution.

There are so-called online content farms, where small armies of writers generate syndicated content, such as articles, in somewhat abbreviated form. They do this to attract traffic, to encourage website owners to participate, and to gain the attention of search engines.

There is opt-in syndication, which relies on Web users to sign up and receive your syndicated content on a regular basis.

Viral syndication is something many dream of achieving. It happens when your content suddenly reaches a massive audience in a short time. If the content is something you want to have distributed, then it's a wonderful thing. It can make you famous overnight.

But if the viral content is, for example, a hidden camera video of you accepting an illegal bribe, then this form of syndication may be your worst nightmare. We'll explore this in the chapter on Internet syndication.

The income stream from online syndication may be unpredictable, or one step removed from the syndication itself. For example, someone might syndicate Web content to drive traffic to their site. The traffic eventually generates income, through visitor ad clicks or product sales. Just be aware that the ad revenue model for online syndicated content is not nearly as well established as it is for radio and TV syndication.

With Web syndication, one must have persistence to deal with all the competition. You also need a truly unique and definable difference that sets you apart from others. Web consumers are able to share content they enjoy with others near and far, providing the benefit of organic audience growth.

We will cover various aspects of Internet syndication and more, in the pages ahead.

Wrapping It Up

You should now have a better idea of the advantages and disadvantages of different forms of media syndication. Keep in mind that you can launch in the medium you prefer and later expand into other media, depending upon your aims and goals.

Forbes magazine recently pointed out that we've entered an era in which there are more entrepreneurial media celebrities than ever before. This is because the modern world has made it possible not only to be the star of your content, but also to own that content— and reap the back-end profits.

Not so many years ago, Oprah Winfrey was one of a very few who had successfully achieved this goal in TV syndication. But today, *Forbes'* Celebrity List contains over 15 super-wealthy celebrity entrepreneurs, whose main income comes from their own businesses—not from networks, record labels, or outside studios. The trend is clear.

If you're someone who wants to control your destiny and be the owner of your media brand, this may be the best time in modern history to make that happen. Later in the book we'll explore this option, along with the concept of founding your own media network.

Chapter 4 – How the Business Began

Knowing a little history can be a valuable thing. So in this chapter, we'll take a quick look back at the beginnings of media syndication, find out how the barter ad system first began, and follow the growth of broadcast syndication into what it is today. We'll also make some educated guesses about what the future holds.

Your first temptation might be to skip over this chapter. You might think that what's done is done, the past is best forgotten, and what happens NOW is what counts. But understanding what came before can help you be more successful today.

For one thing, the pioneers of syndication were clever and resourceful people. You may want to borrow some of their timeless strategies. Secondly, knowing a bit about the errors of the past can help you avoid common mistakes today. Finally, some of the stories of syndication's early days are truly inspiring. You can use them as motivation to fuel your fire.

So skip ahead if you must, but come back later for some valuable lessons you would otherwise miss.

One caveat: This is not meant as a definitive history or scholarly treatise on media syndication. It's simply a collection of facts and stories about what took place before today's well-established syndication scene.

The Earliest Days

Who can say when syndication in its earliest form really began? All that was required for syndication to exist was for someone to create content of wide interest and set up multiple points of distribution for that content. Lost in antiquity is the identity of the first clever publisher who realized the value of syndicating content. No doubt other publishers saw the concept in action, recognized a genius idea, and immediately started copying the formula.

It's an established fact that in the Victorian 1800s (the era of Charles Dickens), writers were paid on an installment basis to crank out multi-chapter serials for publication in newspapers. These installments were syndicated to multiple papers, enabling the content to reach eager readers in many different locales. This was true syndication in a very early form.

If one of those early serial writers was able to keep generating fresh ideas and story lines, then their syndicated newspaper series could continue for years and years. It was in the creator's best interest to keep cranking out high-quality content. The longer a syndicated hit kept running, the more income the writer could earn, and the more papers would get sold. Over time, the fame of the best serial writers grew among the public, leading to new income opportunities for these individuals.

After some of these newspaper serials ran their course, a collection of the stories might later be published in book form. This is an old-time example of a syndicator generating back-end profits (BEP) from the original content!

Some of these Victorian-era print serials in book form are still selling today, more than 100 years after they were first created. Some of these timeless stories have been made into motion pictures, or adapted for use in other media. This demonstrates the perpetual value of original, quality content, long after its first use in syndication. This is something to keep in mind as you consider the copyright and ownership of your content. Who knows? The products you create today might become a valuable legacy for your descendants in the decades ahead.

Newspaper Content

In the late 1800s and early 1900s, news associations were formed to distribute content to papers in multiple markets. Some of these associations were owned by various newspaper chains, and others were independent.

These organizations distributed national and overseas news reports, business and sports statistics, news photos, and other content to local papers on a market-exclusive basis.

Independent papers typically paid a fee to belong to a news association, but there was a considerable cost savings for the paper over staffing their own national and foreign reporters, photographers, business reporters, and others. For example, instead of paying a reporter to cover a war in Europe, a paper could run syndicated reports from an association reporter who was near the battle scene.

Beginning around 1895, print syndicators began using crude telephonic devices to transmit syndicated content, such as photos, to newspapers in major cities. By the early 1900s, more syndicated content was being distributed to newspapers using an early version of a fax machine (the Belinograph). Hence the origin of the terms *wire photo* and *wire story*—which were often shorthand terms for syndicated newspaper content.

Also beginning in the 1890s, one of print syndication's most enduring and beloved hit products first appeared: the comic strip. The early strips included "The Katzenjammer Kids," "Little Orphan Annie," "Mutt & Jeff," and others. A newspaper war between Joseph Pulitzer and William Randolph Hearst helped make comic strips even more popular, as these feisty competitors began printing comics in color and heavily promoting them to readers.

Just as with the newspaper serials of an earlier time, certain comic strips later became valuable long-term properties, generating profits years after their initial print runs. This is still true in modern times, with comics such as "Peanuts" and "Dilbert" generating plenty of BEP.

Tale of a Top Columnist

There were certainly syndicated columnists before Walter Winchell came along, but few of them had his unique flair or his lasting influence on culture. Maybe you've never heard his name. But Winchell was most assuredly the top syndicated columnist of the early and middle 20th century.

There's an excellent biography of the man, *Winchell,* by author Neal Gabler. If your dream is to write a syndicated column, the book is recommended reading.

In his personal life, Winchell wasn't the most admirable man. But if you read between the lines, you'll see how his work ethic and originality helped make him a household name.

Winchell began as a low-rated, struggling performer in vaudeville. He decided to parlay his inside show-biz knowledge into the media, as a vaudeville news reporter. His first job was with a rag called the *Vaudeville News,* for which he wrote a small column. His job functions also included being the newspaper's errand boy and deliverer. He later said that many agents and other industry figures to whom he'd deliver his paper would take it from his hands and throw it directly in the trash.

But he was doggedly persistent. His goal was to write the most "inside" interesting column he could. He constantly plied his news sources for fresh tips. To supplement his income, he began selling the print ads next to his column.

His relentless approach soon got him noticed, and he was hired by a "real" newspaper to write a Broadway column. Rather than relax in this more comfortable perch, the new job inspired him to even greater heights. His standard greeting to everyone was, "What do you know that I don't know?"

His was the first Broadway-only column. Others had written occasional pieces about the Theater District, but Winchell was the first to make it his exclusive niche. In syndication, there's nothing more powerful than owning a niche, and he truly did. Eventually the content evolved into the nation's first celebrity gossip column.

Winchell coined many phrases and created a *slanguage* of his very own, some of which is still in use by today's gossip columnists. One example is "thisclose," as in "the romantic duo was thisclose." He also used code phrases, such as "(name) is expecting a blessed event," rather than making the potentially libelous claim that someone was pregnant. Winchell constantly bounced ideas off others for feedback, before using the bits in print.

Syndication Made Him a Star

His popular column was a hit in syndication. It first appeared in papers in every big U.S. city, and later in most small towns, too. His daily column was the first thing many Americans turned to when they read the paper.

Newspaper syndication made Walter Winchell a major national celebrity. It led to a book contract from Simon and Schuster, and countless profiles in national magazines.

Winchell's growing success took him to radio. He began hosting a live, nightly national broadcast consisting of hot gossip, news items, and commentary. His famous sign-on (accompanied by urgent telegraph beeps) was "Good evening, Mr. and Mrs. America and all the ships at sea. Let's go to press!" He then read his scripted content in a rapid-fire, staccato style, still mimicked today.

At the height of his fame, he even starred in a Hollywood movie.

Although his fame was fading by the 1960s, Winchell did the narration for "The Untouchables" TV drama series for five years.

Lessons to Learn

So what can we learn from Walter Winchell, when it comes to syndication?

Number one: You do not need connections or wealth to begin. What you do need is a niche topic you understand. It must be something you feel passionate about sharing with others. Then you need to start somewhere—anywhere. Winchell began at a lowly newspaper.

Number two: Don't get discouraged when your content isn't accepted right away. Recall that many industry leaders threw Winchell's early content right into the trash. Stay focused and be very persistent.

Number three: Be creative and unique, and break the mold. But it's wise to test new ideas on others you trust, before taking them national. Winchell literally created his own words and phrases to keep his column fresh and interesting.

Number four: When making the jump to other media, don't just re-hash what you already do. Come up with a fresh, different approach, as Winchell did with his radio show. In fact, I suspect that if someone today were to adapt the intro, trappings, and energy of Winchell's radio show with updated content, it might capture a significant audience.

Golden Radio Days

Now let's explore a little broadcasting history.

The 1920s was the decade when commercial radio burst onto the national scene. KDKA Pittsburgh led the way, signing on in November 1920. From that auspicious beginning, new stations began appearing weekly. All those new outlets needed plenty of content to fill their airwaves.

In the early years, most stations came up with original, local programs such as musical concerts, church broadcasts, sporting events, children's programs, and so on. Many of the outlets signed off each day for a number of hours, due in part to a lack of programming. But it wasn't long before enterprising radio producers began offering stations syndicated content.

By the late 1920s, radio networks began to appear. Similar to the news associations that distributed print content and images to many newspapers, radio nets were formed to provide multiple radio stations with audio content. Much of this content consisted of live entertainment shows originating from studios in New York, Chicago, or Los Angeles. They were distributed nationwide by established networks, using telephone lines connected to affiliate stations.

The largest of these networks were NBC and CBS. NBC soon grew so dominant that anti-trust regulators split it into two parts, known as the Red Network and the Blue Network. The Blue Network eventually became the American Broadcasting Company, otherwise known as ABC.

Independent Distribution

Independent syndicators in radio's early days, such as the Detroit-based producer of "The Lone Ranger" dramatic series, could not justify the huge expense of forming a wired network for their single show. Nor did they want to hand over the rights to their popular show by joining an existing network.

The solution for most independents was to use transcription discs for distribution. These were a fragile forerunner of the vinyl phonograph record.

First, the weekly show was produced and edited into a master recording. Then, the delicate discs were duplicated, labeled, carefully packaged, and shipped directly to radio stations. Since there was no automation in those days, each disc had to be recorded manually, typewritten labels had to be glued to each disc, and each disc set had to be prepared for delivery. Despite all the labor involved, this system worked well for hundreds of syndicated shows over many years.

In fact, thanks to all those transcription discs, many episodes of old-time radio shows survived for us to enjoy today.

The method of shipping recording discs containing syndicated radio content was so effective that it was still being used for station distribution as recently as the 1980s!

Barter Beginnings

In traditional media syndication, there are two basic ways to receive value from the local outlets that carry your content. The first is to have outlets pay cash for the content.

The second is known as "barter." When you barter your content, the outlets will trade you something of value in exchange for the content. In most cases, what you get in the trade is advertising time on the outlet, which can be quite valuable.

In fact, barter is today the most common way that modern radio and TV syndicators are compensated for their shows. We'll explore barter in more depth in later chapters.

But back in radio's olden, golden days, business terms weren't standardized. A syndicated show might require payment of cash, or cash plus barter, or even third-party barter terms including merchandise or services.

Story of a Syndication Salesman

Marv Kempner has had a long and colorful career in syndication, first in radio and then in television. His primary role was selling programs to stations. Later, he owned his own syndication company. In 1998 he wrote a book about it, titled *Can't Wait Till Monday Morning*.

In a recent interview, the still-spry 89-year-old shared a few stories with us about those days.

Kempner's first office was a phone booth in New York City, where he would make an endless string of calls until he got an appointment to see someone at a local station. Then he'd rush over to the prospect's office and ask them to buy radio jingles from his company. This approach actually worked for him, while teaching him a lot about how to get decision-makers on the phone.

That led him into selling syndicated content to radio stations nationwide. One of his first shows was a sports feature with baseball manager Joe McCarthy. Later, there were music shows and other radio products. Kempner learned that the best way to begin the syndication process for a new product was to sign up small and medium markets. This established a base of stations for the new show. Then, he'd go after the major markets, one by one.

The reason for this strategy? Major markets do not want to be proving grounds for new syndication. They want to see a list of stations across the U.S. already on board. Proof of industry acceptance made it less risky for the majors to add a show. The same holds true today.

Kempner told us that back then, radio barter was unheard of for most products. Everything he did was on a strict cash basis with stations.

He also explained to us that one of the most popular syndicated radio products in the 1940s and early 1950s were radio "libraries." These were large collections of music or spoken word content on custom record discs, tailored to appeal to a specific age group of listeners. Let's say a certain station catered to upscale adults. In that case, a syndicated library they'd want to buy might contain instrumental, easy listening tunes.

It was bland content for the most part, but stations of that era bought libraries like crazy. Even the networks got into the library game. As Kempner explained, the "NBC Library" was one of the most popular syndicated radio products at that time.

This gave him the idea of creating a library of commercial jingles, which could be used to enhance a station's local ad sales. For example, a singing jingle might be "Shop with us for the best bargains!" The chosen jingle would be added to a client's radio spot, to jazz it up. The product was a sensation, and Marv sold hundreds of the jingle libraries to stations. No doubt something like this would still work well today.

The Ziv Empire

In the early 1950s, a man named Fred Ziv ran a small Cincinnati ad agency. He'd noticed the rising demand for syndicated products at radio stations. So Fred took some associates with him on the road to sell a package of slick, pre-produced radio commercials that stations could instantly use to sign up clients. These sold very well to stations all over the country.

But Fred's next move was revolutionary.

Most radio syndicators of that era (as well as today's) start out by trying to sell their program directly to stations. Fred turned the process upside-down by first selling his syndicated content to a big national advertiser. Since it was pre-sold, stations rarely refused to carry it.

Fred Ziv accomplished this difficult task by recruiting a big-name talent, such as a Hollywood star, as the featured talent. Then, he'd produce a show of superb quality featuring the famous star.

Next, Fred and his team would put on a fancy dog and pony show for a national advertiser, dazzling them with the idea of sponsoring such an impressive radio show.

Based upon Fred's guarantee that he would get the show placed on a minimum number of stations, the sponsor would sign up and hand over the first of several big checks. Once this happened, Fred Ziv's sales work was all done.

Fred's next easy step was to invest the initial sponsor funds to buy blocks of airtime on many radio stations to carry the show, which fulfilled his guarantee. What about the rest of the sponsor funds? That money was pure profit for Ziv.

As Marv Kempner explained to us, sometimes a sponsor would decide they didn't like being the sponsor of one of Ziv's shows, after it had run for a few weeks. But when they'd try canceling, they'd hit a legal brick wall. This was because the sponsor had signed Ziv's iron-clad contract.

Start of Television Syndication

Thanks to Ziv's winning track record in radio syndication, he was ready when TV came along. Ziv Television quickly became the dominant syndicator of the new medium. They followed the very same strategy of using big-name talent to market their TV syndicated programming. Eventually, Fred Ziv sold his company and retired a wealthy man.

1955 Ziv Television syndication advertisement

However, Kempner says the first real groundbreaking syndication deal in TV was done by a man named Matty Fox. Fox was an expert negotiator. He managed to convince Howard Hughes to license him the entire RKO movie library for television use. The library consisted of nearly 800 full-length feature films.

Back in the mid-1950s, TV stations were desperate for any kind of content to fill their airtime. But most Hollywood studios were very reluctant to help the new competitor, so the studio's film vaults were off-limits to the medium.

Matty Fox would ride to the stations' rescue—for a price.

In fact, he already had a client eager to sponsor his syndicated film library. The client was Playtex, a manufacturer of women's undergarments. They agreed to pay the huge sum of $21 million to be the exclusive national sponsor of the TV movie package.

Having pulled off two outrageous deals already—first with Howard Hughes and then with Playtex—Matty Fox came up with one more. In fact, his next move was brilliant.

Barter Bonanza

As Marv explained to us, Matty offered the entire RKO film library to stations for a minimum term of five years, and in some cases up to seven years, on a market exclusive basis.

Best of all, it wouldn't cost the stations a penny! All they had to do was run a schedule of Playtex commercials from morning until night, every day, for five to seven years. What a bargain! Stations in almost every U.S. market quickly signed the binding deal.

Matty then pocketed a large chunk of the $21 million, after paying RKO its film library licensing fee. Kempner said it was the biggest barter deal ever done in television.

Pioneer TV stations had little or no experience in barter syndication. So they had no clue what they'd just agreed to with Matty Fox. But they soon realized their fate, when they had to schedule and run all those thousands of barter spots selling women's undergarments.

The TV commercials for Playtex were on the air constantly, day and night, from early morning through prime time, month after month, year after year, for as long as seven years. This was in an era when TV ads began to soar in value. Yet these stations were locked into a massive barter commitment. They couldn't fully cash in on the growing demand for TV ads, with all the trade spots they'd handed over to Playtex.

In the end, Playtex received many, many times the value in ad time, compared to the relatively meager $21 million they'd invested. In fact, trade magazines of the time estimated the actual airtime Playtex received at almost $250 million! And clever Matty Fox walked away with a bundle.

Radio Barter Begins

Outrageous syndication deals are rare these days, simply because everyone involved is more sophisticated than in the early days.

But Kempner believes the infamous RKO-Playtex deal was an inspiration for the entire broadcasting industry. New barter ad firms soon began appearing. Some traded airtime on stations in exchange for programming, while others traded airtime for hard goods. This was the era when barter began to be accepted in radio syndication.

Since the early days of barter syndication, the business has evolved dramatically. Today, digital distribution of content is the norm. Most marketing of syndication is now done by phone, email, and the Web. However, the basic process of radio and TV syndication has not changed significantly. Content is delivered to stations in exchange for barter ad inventory. This system has been viable for decades, right up to the present. It will likely continue indefinitely, because it works so well for stations, syndicators, and advertisers.

You may be wondering why stations are willing to barter their airtime, and why a syndicator wants to have the barter minutes. We'll explain that in a later chapter.

Growth Signs and Statistics

What's the status of traditional broadcast media in today's world? Commercial radio has been around for over 90 years. Despite its age, it's still growing.

A recent Arbitron research study shows that radio's total national audience jumped by over 2 million weekly radio listeners, compared to the previous two years. The total number of people over 12 years of age now using radio each week exceeds 240 million—about 93% of the U.S. population. And the study showed that radio reaches nearly 95% of adults 18-49 years of age who have a household income of at least $75,000. Network radio listening is growing, too.

Despite the overall audience growth, many stations do not have the budgets they once did to support a full schedule of locally produced programming. So what do they do? Stations now use more and more radio syndication to fill their airwaves.

According to Arbitron and Edison Research, the daily time that consumers spend with TV, radio, and the Internet (combined) has grown by a remarkable 20% in the last decade. In fact, today's consumers spend an average of 8 hours and 11 minutes per day with these media, compared to just 6 hours and 50 minutes per day ten years ago.

Looking at TV alone, the Nielsen Company reports that broadcast TV still outperforms cable when it comes to audience. A top-rated network TV show can garner a weekly audience of perhaps 20 million, while a top-rated cable show might pull in 6 million per week. Although TV viewing overall is down from previous years, this is still a very impressive number.

What about TV syndication? A top-rated syndicated show, such as "Wheel of Fortune," can attract over 10 million viewers a week.

Newspapers are experiencing an overall decline in readership, primarily due to competition from new media. From 2010 to 2011, the Audit Bureau of Circulations reports that U.S. newspaper readership fell by about 8.5%.

The Internet is the fastest growing of all media. According to Internet World Stats, nearly 205 million Americans now use the Internet. U.S. users grew by an impressive 146% from 2000 to 2010. And over the same period, Web use in the rest of the world jumped 572%, to a total of 1.7 billion users.

What the Future May Hold

Does history repeat itself? If so, what does this mean for syndication?

If the Victorian era of syndication gives us any clue, chances are people will be consuming syndicated content decades (and perhaps centuries) from now.

The means for media delivery and consumption may change as technology evolves, but solid content will always be in demand, judging from the past 100+ years of syndication.

As with the advent of television syndication, new media can cause marketplace disruption, creating new opportunities and deal making. This is still true with the Internet. As new forms of media come about in the future, there will surely be more opportunities for savvy entrepreneurs.

Some Things Never Change

Certainly, people will always want to read, listen to, and view content of all kinds. It only makes sense that the creators and producers of quality content should try to distribute it through as many means as possible, in order to reach the maximum possible number of media consumers.

Beyond that broad prediction, it's difficult to guess accurately what will happen to the present forms of media. We know that at present, traditional broadcast media (radio and television) continue to deliver mass audiences.

Some say that radio may see a decline when live Internet streaming becomes widely accessible in cars, since car listening remains a radio stronghold. Yet a recent study of early adopters of automobile Internet streaming showed that drivers continue to favor traditional radio, despite the availability of Web streams in their cars.

And while Internet radio listening is growing by leaps and bounds, traditional radio continues to show healthy audience growth, as well.

Television lost its exclusive perch as the purveyor of video when cable TV arrived on the scene. Now, Web video, DVRs, smart phones, and a host of new video-delivery platforms and upstart networks are competing for viewers. But despite technology's onslaught, traditional TV still delivers audiences in the tens of millions.

The Internet's rate of growth will certainly slow as the market approaches saturation. But new and innovative Web content distribution ideas will undoubtedly keep popping up.

Newspapers may face a difficult future, as they transition to digital delivery and away from the old formats. Yet the top papers still maintain large followings of loyal readers, and well-run small town newspapers still connect with subscribers.

Whatever the future may hold, it's a sure bet that syndication will continue to play a key role in the media landscape.

Chapter 5 – Select Your Specialty

With syndication as your goal, one of the first keys to success is selecting a niche you are interested in dominating. It should be a topic or an area of focus that inspires and interests you. Your passion for the topic will come through in the content you create, which will help you attract and build an audience. It's also worth noting that as your syndication audience grows, you may be living with this topic for a long time—perhaps for the rest of your life!

For these reasons, it's best to choose a niche topic you find truly fascinating, not just one you think might make you lots of money.

Owning a Niche

Let's face it. No matter how broad and varied your interests may be, you can't encompass them all in your syndication content. In fact, nobody can. So it only makes sense for you to try to become THE expert at ONE thing.

Whether you plan to write a syndicated column, host a syndicated music or talk show on radio, produce a syndicated TV show, or create syndicated Web content, owning a niche will make your quest for success far easier.

Some readers might want to debate this point. They might claim that some generalists have made it big in syndication. For example, Oprah Winfrey might fall into this category, since her syndicated TV show covered many topics, with guests from all walks of life. But it could also be argued that Oprah actually did own a niche—specifically, that of "America's daytime TV talk show personality." In fact, Oprah was the dominant market leader in this niche. So a niche can be content-driven or format-driven.

Here's a radio example of a format-driven program. Mike Carruthers first learned about syndication when he was control room engineer for the late Top 40 radio legend Robert W. Morgan. Morgan's syndicated show was "The Record Report," a daily 90-

second feature. In each show, Morgan shared a little-known story about a rock musician. Carruthers thought the format was good, but guessed that many listeners found stories about musicians tedious. So Carruthers created and voiced his own 90-second feature, which reveals little-known facts about the world at large. His program, "Something You Should Know," still airs on 150 stations. Carruther's topics are always general in nature, but he dominates the category of short, general information radio features.

By and large, it's the specialists that rule the roost when it comes to syndication success. This is why I suggest you strive to be the best at one specific thing.

Even if your goal is to do a radio talk show on conservative politics (for example), and you have little hope of outdoing the leader in this category (Rush Limbaugh), there are ways you can make yourself unique and different from Rush and all the other conservative talkers. In this way, you not only differentiate yourself from the category leader; you also stand out from others in a crowded market niche.

Passion over Competition

No matter what type of syndicated content you wish to distribute, here's one easy rule to remember: Passion beats competition.

The previous chapter briefly profiled columnist Walter Winchell, who rose from total obscurity and near-poverty to become the leading nationally syndicated newspaper columnist of the mid-20th century. His intensity and drive were far greater than his competitors'. This is what first got him noticed, and later helped him to become well established.

When the inevitable copycats and competitors sprang up, Winchell out-hustled them and continued to innovate, which kept him on top. It was his passion that helped him beat the others cold.

Be a Money Attractor

A common question that beginners often ask is how to find sponsors or investors to fund their syndication effort and help pay the bills.

You'll find it easier to attract funding if you are viewed as a top expert in your niche category. No matter where your starting line may be, make it your goal to learn virtually everything you can about your niche topic, or to be the very best at dominating your niche format. Then find the most effective ways to provide that content to your audience, in an entertaining way.

Notice that we did not say, "be THE top expert," because that may be an impossible task. There might be recognized geniuses with advanced degrees on the subject. Others may have devoted their entire lives to studying your topic. Some niche gurus may have staffs of research assistants, or rows of powerful computers packed with data on the topic.

But being viewed as a top expert is a matter of perception. When it comes to the media, perception is often reality. To be seen as a top expert, never give your audience the impression you are winging it. Just the opposite, in fact. Learn all you can and constantly expand your knowledge of your niche. Interview as many experts as you can, and try to be a clearinghouse of solid information. If possible, get a few experts to endorse your work. Consider writing a book about your favorite topic, because a published author is deemed to "have written the book" on their area of expertise.

As you start becoming recognized as a real authority in your niche, you will have more credibility when you contact moneyed interests. Advertisers in your niche may even reach out to you first, because the mantle of authority you wear can make you stand out as an opinion leader in your category. At the very least, potential sponsors will be open to your inquiries. Your position as a leader will help convince them that you offer a solid platform for marketing their products and services.

Finding Your Ideal Nest

Perhaps you already know exactly what niche topic you want for your syndicated content. But if you're still unsure, or just need some help focusing your ideas, this next section may be useful.

The first question to ask yourself is a simple one: What do people tend to compliment you on? It might be something that you consider quite ordinary. Perhaps you cook a fabulous breakfast, or you always seem to know about the latest music or movies. Maybe you've done a great job of decorating your home. Are you a smart investor, or do you know a lot about cars? The possibilities are endless, because everyone is unique and special in certain ways.

Don't automatically dismiss what others say about your particular talent or area of expertise. You might think something you do is unimportant or trivial, or you may believe that your knowledge about a topic is quite commonplace. But if others have said that you stand out in a certain way, heed what they're saying. Their words might hold important clues for your future.

Spend some time pondering your natural-born talents and abilities. Sadly, most people never bother to do this, once they get settled in a career. Their choice for a work path may have been influenced by outside forces, such as parental pressure, school advisors, what a friend thought was "cool," or just simple economics. As a result, what they do for a living may have little to do with their natural abilities and interests.

It stands to reason that if you're really interested in something, you'll easily spend many happy hours intently focused on that thing. An example is our early fascination with the radio business—we couldn't get enough of it. This level of involvement is a great advantage when it comes to ensuring your career success, your income growth, and your overall level of enjoyment.

Here's one way to rediscover your inborn talents and abilities. Think back to your childhood years. Every kid naturally spends hours doing what they love most. Again, consider everything that comes to mind. We suggest you make a list on paper. Do not dismiss any of your childhood fascinations, thinking they no longer apply to the "real world" of adulthood.

Consider this example: A boy grew up with a passion for comic books and fantasy stories. He'd save every penny of his weekly allowance to go to the movies on Saturdays. The rest of the time, he did little more than daydream about imaginary worlds. His father reportedly told others, "This kid will amount to nothing!"

You may wonder how anyone could turn such trivial interests into a worthwhile career. But that boy grew up to become incredibly wealthy, and you know his name: George Lucas. He's the creator of *Star Wars*, *Indiana Jones*, and much more. Lucas's success came from doing exactly what he loved best, and your success can come about in the same way.

The Medium Sets Your Focus

As you make your plans to syndicate, what medium and what format will you choose? These factors will affect how deeply you can delve into your ideal topic, as well as how sharply defined your niche presentation will be.

Let's say you go into syndication as Mike Carruthers did, with a short daily vignette, brief sound-bite interview, or how-to tip. In this format, there's not much time or space for you to elaborate on the chosen subject. However, I like to think of short, recurring content as the proverbial "water dripping on a rock."

Day after day, week after week, that content slowly reveals great power. Just as drops of water can eventually wear through solid granite, so will your daily stream of content eventually get you noticed and recognized as a real expert. However, you won't have much time on any given day to delve very deeply into the topic of your choice.

Tight and Right

Some advice regarding the narrowness of your focus: If you plan to syndicate to traditional mass media such as radio or television, remember that it is called "broadcasting" for a reason.

You don't want your content to be so narrow that you lose portions of the general audience. On the other hand, you also should avoid being a generalist, because you'll lose whatever makes your show special and unique. You must strike the right balance.

At times, you may be able to drill down and get very tight with your focus, as long as you don't dwell too long on that tight point of view. For example, let's say you plan to create a syndicated TV show about gourmet cooking. You happen to have a special fascination with desserts and pastries (and who doesn't?). But if you spend most of the show talking about desserts, you'll quickly kill the show's overall theme, gourmet cooking. You may also start losing portions of your mass audience, because they were drawn to the broader topic of gourmet cooking—not just desserts.

So a dessert show on broadcast TV might be too narrow a topic. However, there may well be room on cable TV (or the Web) for video content with a narrow food focus. Again, the medium decides the message to a significant extent.

Web Topic Options

If you choose to syndicate your content on the Internet, be aware that this is a different animal from traditional media. If you wish, you can zoom all the way in on your topic and command a highly specific niche. In fact, doing this online may be to your advantage. Since so much Web content is available from so many different creators, being super-focused may make it easier for a niche audience to find you and relate to you.

Keep in mind that if you follow the approach of very narrow topic definition, your total audience will likely be smaller than it might be otherwise. But that audience will tend to be more hardcore when it comes to their interest in the niche topic.

Credibility and Content

If you want to get noticed and make a positive impact on the world around you, content creation is king. Quality content will work hard for you, informing and entertaining others, giving them your message and point of view. Depending on the medium, you can deliver your content live and/or in recorded or written form. Your content can reach consumers around the clock, if you wish. It can be enjoyed by consumers today, tomorrow, and possibly for months or years to come.

But creating your content is only part of the deal. Once you've got the content, you need to distribute it to as large an audience as you possibly can. As you've already realized, syndication is a great way to reach the nation. It's the difference between putting your message on paper handbills and handing them out to passersby in an alley, versus putting your message up in big, bold letters on a giant illuminated billboard next to the busiest expressway in town.

As you make plans to get your message on a big national platform, be certain you know your stuff. At the very least, know it well enough to feel confident about it. Avoid trying to syndicate content on any topic or concept you're unsure about. Material that contains inaccuracies or is hastily thrown together is bad news. You always want to give it your very best shot.

Watch Your Standards

Being on 100 or more radio or TV stations, on 500 websites, or in dozens of newspapers will definitely give your content real impact. If your presentation is solid and you consistently put out high-quality stuff for your audience, you'll get results that will be rewarding.

But if you let your standards slip badly just once, by releasing sloppy content that is full of errors—or worse, that contains libel or slander—there's no taking it back once it reaches that mass audience. Winging it can put your credibility at risk with consumers, as well as with the gatekeepers who place your syndicated content on their media outlets.

We're sure you recall some of the "famous personality flameouts" that periodically make the headlines. They seem to happen without warning. All it takes is for someone that the news media considers fairly notable to make a bad slip in public. It can happen on the air, in print, or even at some public venue. Perhaps this person said something that came across as too personal, too antagonistic, or too divisive. Maybe he or she crossed a line and offended segments of the audience. Or maybe it was just a dumb factual error.

When such a slip-up happens, the modern 24/7 news cycle can be unforgiving. On a slow news day, the gaffe may be replayed endlessly, magnifying the story for millions who never heard of the offender in the first place. In a matter of hours, a talented personality can have his or her reputation badly tarnished.

This scenario should not worry you. The fact is, quality syndicated content is cranked out by the ton every day, and enjoyed by countless millions of people. Problems like these occur only when a content creator or media personality makes a blunder. Perhaps they tried guessing, rather than admit to the audience they didn't know something. Or they opened their mouth before engaging their brain. Or they simply let their emotions run away with them, and blurted something into an open microphone.

Being on target with your niche topic is important, but never put your reputation and all your hard work at risk by ignoring sensible cautions.

Niche Competition

Regardless of the subject or focus of your show, there will probably be others with similar interests trying to reach an audience similar to yours.

Maybe you believe you host the only syndicated radio show about Estonian basket weaving, anywhere. But it's a sure bet that somebody else is doing that topic, too. Maybe they have a podcast or blog on the subject. It's unavoidable in this fractured media world.

We believe there will always competition, no matter what the niche. If you don't think you have any competition at present, it probably just means you haven't discovered it yet. The fact is, we live in a very small world.

And when your Estonian basket weaving radio show becomes a success in syndication, you can definitely expect similar syndicated products to pop up on the same topic. It's the nature of the media: Success breeds copycats and spin-offs.

As someone who has experienced this kind of very direct competition with my first syndicated show, let me predict what you reactions will be when you learn of a copycat.

Step Up Your Game

First, you'll think they have a lot of nerve, trying to horn in on your territory. Next, you'll look for ways to step up your game, to create an even better product to better fend them off. (If the new player is savvy, they'll try to do the same.) This is the beauty of competition: It keeps making things better for consumers.

But assuming you began with a good product and you work at staying on top, chances are good you'll remain on top and the others will keep following you.

In our case, there were a string of competitors who figured the show we'd created (a daily profile of a successful person or brand name, with a surprise twist ending) would be easy to copy. At one point, there were four similar shows on the market! But one by one, they seem to have dropped out. Our show is still going strong, nearly 20 years later. We believe this is mainly because it was the first with this unique approach to this niche topic, and also because we kept up the quality of the product.

Setbacks Are Inevitable

Over the years, we've interviewed many successful people. We've learned something that applies to everyone, especially in syndication: There are no straight lines to the top. There will always be setbacks. Competitors come and go, problems happen along the way, and you will have ups and downs. You may think somebody famous was an overnight success, but when you study them, you learn about their many failures along the way.

Early on we made a point of tracking our syndication growth, using a big wall chart. We studied that chart every day. The line was anything but smooth. It was more like the jagged EKG chart of a heart patient. And no wonder—we had a few heart-pounding moments (both good and bad) along the way. Keep a clear vision of what you are working toward and you'll ride out the inevitable ups and downs of the syndication growth process, as you grow to become a true leader in your niche specialty.

Chapter 6 – You and Your Audience

Now let's turn to the all-important relationship between you and your audience. First we'll explore why an audience might want the content that only you can give them. Then we'll delve into ways you can best connect with consumers and turn them into loyal, long-term fans.

A Common Problem

Over the many years we have been in syndication consulting, we've been contacted by a countless number of people. Each of them had a special dream of syndicating their content to a mass audience. All of these people had in one way or another glimpsed the vast potential of syndication to transform their lives, and the lives of others, for the better.

Most of them could easily see the potential rewards of putting themselves and their message in front of a national audience.

But a common problem that plagued many of them was doubt—in some cases, crippling doubt. Many of them struggled to visualize themselves winning in syndication. Often it seemed easier for them to make a few halfhearted attempts at starting up, rather than jumping in with both feet and pursuing their dream wholeheartedly.

For example, some would eagerly gather lots of information about the process, but then decide syndication was just too audacious a goal to achieve. And they would walk away from their dream.

We consider these lost opportunities, not only for the content creators who failed to pursue their dreams, but also for their potential audiences—who missed out on the interesting content each of those syndicators might have provided.

What Audiences Want

Here is something to consider, if and when doubts begin to gnaw at you.

Let's assume you have high-quality, compelling content to share with a mass audience. And let's also assume you believe that your product will entertain, inform, and inspire others. If these assumptions are correct, then the only thing that can stop you from syndicating yourself in at least one medium is your own inaction. And that's a fact.

It's very likely there are consumers who right this moment are seeking good quality content of the kind that YOU can provide.

After reading that last sentence, you may be wondering something. Since not everyone has "good quality content" to syndicate, how can it be true that everyone's got a national audience waiting to get their stuff?

Well, here's the startling truth that many overlook. Your definition and my definition of "good quality content" may be far different from what millions of others consider to be "good quality content."

Let us consider two extreme examples to illustrate this. Do you recall a TV show called "Hee Haw"? For those unfamiliar, it was a cornball variety show based in a fictional setting known as Kornfield Kounty. The series was savaged by critics for its inane, hick level of comedy.

Despite the criticism, "Hee Haw" ran for 20 years in syndication. It earned a vast fortune for its creators. Not only was it a big hit in medium markets, but it also pulled solid ratings in "sophisticated" markets like New York and Los Angeles when it was syndicated.

At the polar opposite of TV's intellectual spectrum is "Masterpiece Theater." This highbrow PBS show recently celebrated its 40th season and it remains hugely popular. Episodes are seen in syndication.

Something for Everyone

The point is, the total national audience is truly massive. No one can hope to attract 100% of the entire media audience in any way, shape, or form. But within that vast totality, there are large chunks of audience that have widely varied tastes, income levels, and interests. That's why we believe there's a sizable audience out there for virtually any content of good quality—no matter what your personal definition of "good quality" may be.

Despite this reality, self-doubt remains a roadblock for many who have a dream of syndication. So let's explore why the unique content that only you can create may be in demand right now.

The Entertainment Factor

When was the last time you went online, listened to radio, watched TV, or read a print publication? Odds are, it was within the last few hours. Most Americans enjoy spending lots of time with media. For heavy media consumers, virtually all of their waking hours involve the Web, television, radio, reading, or some combination thereof. Why is rampant media consumption such an ingrained habit for so many?

For one thing, media provides a doorway to the world. It tells us what others are talking about and what others are thinking. It can reassure us that our particular place in the world remains secure— for the moment, anyway. It tells us what parts of the world are in turmoil. It can help to fulfill our needs for personal security, social status, and economic survival in this complex world.

And then there's the universal desire for entertainment. It may not be true that "girls just want to have fun," but it's an irrefutable fact that people want to be entertained. Entertainment provides escape from boredom and relief from stress. For many, a little entertainment and fun are what make life itself worth living.

In ancient Rome, it was said that the populace just wanted "bread and circuses" (in other words, food and fun), and that politicians should find ways to pay for it, while taking care of the problems. Some might say this thinking still rings true today.

Former *Tonight Show* host Johnny Carson once said, "People will pay more to be entertained than they'll pay to be educated," and we believe he was right.

Fun and Facts

But why should there be a big divide between entertainment and education? There are ways to make the learning process very entertaining. Learners can be amused and delighted, just as they might be with mindless entertainment. The difference is, when you combine entertainment with learning, your audience benefits long term. It's actually a powerful way to inform and educate a mass audience, without boring them or causing them to turn away.

Walt Disney was a master of the "fun and facts" combination, both in his documentary films and at his theme parks.

Pleasure Centers

Recently we interviewed a professor of neurology from Johns Hopkins, who had some interesting research findings to share. In every human brain are the so-called pleasure centers. These clusters of neurons fire whenever we experience any sense pleasure, including sex, drugs, and alcohol. The surprising new finding is that the consumption of new media, which in effect is learning something new, fires the same neurons. In other words, humans experience a level of sense pleasure from the intake of fresh information. It seems logical that our brains would be designed this way. Making it pleasurable to absorb new content can help ensure our long-term survival.

Unfortunately, many people grow bored quickly. This is where a strong entertainment factor can make a difference. Successful syndicators understand this, and use it to their advantage.

The most popular talk-show hosts on radio and TV strive to combine witty jokes, snappy commentary, and other entertaining stuff, while presenting their viewpoint. This encourages loyal fans to tune in every day or every week, but not just for the plain old content. They come back because the host combines entertainment with the information.

Meanwhile, a traditional politician gives a dry policy speech and people nod right off. The difference is the entertainment factor. It's a potent way to keep people coming back to your content on a long-term basis.

Tribal Behavior

Let's face it, people are social animals. We are driven to be around other people, to mirror others' behavior, and to seek others' approval and attention.

Honestly answer this question: Do you think that you alone decided on your present wardrobe, your hairstyle, the car you drive, your career path, or even the words and phrases you often say? Unless you're one of a relatively few unique people on Earth, it's a sure bet that all these choices you made were heavily influenced by others.

We're sure you agree that most of us want to be admired and respected by others. We want to be seen as attractive. And just about all of us hope to fit in and be accepted by others at some level. These underlying motivations lead us to dress in certain ways, to purchase one brand over another, and even to choose certain words in our daily conversations.

Even if you still reject the idea that you have been personally influenced by your "tribe" in so many ways, we're guessing you believe most others are affected this way.

Followers Are Everywhere

Studies show that in virtually all human societies, there is a 5 to 95 ratio in effect. Specifically, 5% of the people influence the remaining 95%. Followers aren't found only on Facebook. They are dominant in every society.

These dominance hierarchies are found throughout the nation and the world. You see them in families, in workplaces, in tribal clans, in religions, and in political groups. Wherever groups of people gather, you'll notice there are always a few people leading and a lot of others following. And most everyone is perfectly comfortable with this arrangement.

What does this signify when it comes to an audience wanting your content? Simply this: If you are willing to get out there and passionately state what you believe in, loudly and clearly, you will be seen as a leader in your category. You will then probably be surprised by how many like-minded people notice you, line up behind you, and begin to follow you.

This doesn't apply just to politics, sports, or other "us against them" types of syndicated content, either. Let's say you syndicate a weekly radio show featuring the very latest country music. You make it clear to your audience that you not only respect and love the music, but you want to present the freshest, best quality country tunes available on the planet, better than anyone else on radio. Your forceful, passionate point of view will no doubt find favor with a lot of country music fans—who will follow you and become your loyal tribe.

It's just human nature. You can help nurture this tribal process, by giving your fans the ability to join a website, wear apparel that sports your brand name, and so on.

Handle with Caution

We feel the need here to advise against misusing the tribal effect. You should never mislead or take advantage of anyone who jumps on your bandwagon.

Sometimes, a powerful platform like syndication can be intoxicating. Becoming a national figure can present opportunities to take advantage of others. One such example is a former financial host, who is now serving a lengthy jail term for defrauding some of his most loyal fans. Always use your position as a leader positively, and treat your audience with the respect they deserve.

Early Adopters

Most human beings are naturally inclined to seek and follow a leader. Everyone likes to watch a parade. Taking that one step further, everybody loves to be IN one! Start your own big parade and watch others start to follow you. No doubt there's an audience ready and waiting for you to lead them to something.

But what if you're just starting out and you don't yet have a big audience or a loyal group of followers? That's when you must appeal to the so-called early adopters.

The early adopters in any medium are those who are constantly searching for what's new and different. They are the channel flippers, button pushers, Web surfers, and newsstand junkies. Once you catch their attention and give them something worth sticking around for, they will help spread the good word about you to others. What you must do is provide them with good content and keep it coming.

You can help make your first set of followers experience a real sense of discovery when they initially find your syndicated content. There are many ways to do this, both subtle and overt.

It's worth going out of your way to delight your early adopters. This might require extra personal attention on your part to encourage and thank these special consumers for being there. Reward them in every way possible for joining your tribe and spreading the word. Don't hold back your best content for later, either. Give it to your early adopters now. Then be sure you ask them for their feedback. Be responsive to whatever they may tell you.

Request and publish testimonials from the initial followers. Testimonials will encourage others to sample your content, but you'll also find that everyone who gives you a testimonial will feel their participation has been affirmed. This is natural, because when somebody speaks out in support, their participation reinforces their positive feelings.

Start with a Solid Base

Make it easy for early adopters to share you with others. Facilitate pass-along recommendations using social media. This is a good way to spread the word to new consumers. Your goal should be to build a solid base of enthusiastic fans and grow from there. The initial base of fans can help you grow much faster, if you handle things properly from the start.

Remember, early fans can also become early foes. Don't take them for granted or fail to live up to your promises. Bend over backwards to super-serve this core group.

Meanwhile, don't get too carried away with content development. What I mean is, stay one step ahead of your early adopters with fresh content—but not two steps ahead! Otherwise, you run the risk of losing them or confusing them.

If you follow these steps to solidly interest your initial group of followers and keep them engaged, you'll find many becoming ardent evangelists.

Also, there are small ways to acknowledge your early adopters' special status. For example, you might make them "diamond members" of your website, or send them a special gift. Perks like these will encourage these pioneers to stick around for the long term, as your audience expands.

Help Dreams Come True

Everyone has goals they hope to achieve. It might be finding the perfect mate, getting out of debt, earning a million dollars, electing a great president, starting a new career, seeing a certain team win a championship, finding spiritual fulfillment, raising great kids, and the list goes on.

If your syndicated content can help a segment of the population achieve their dream goal, then you've got a built-in audience ready for what you can give them.

Most consumers ask, "What's in it for me?" But your followers will already know the exact answer to that question. They will naturally follow you because you hold the keys to the goal they seek.

Fulfill Their Trust

Once these goal-oriented folks discover you, all you have to do is fulfill their trust on an ongoing basis. Do that, and most will remain loyal and invite others to join your audience.

How do you fulfill trust in this instance? By giving your audience regular doses of realistic, meaningful how-to content that they can apply and use in practical ways. They can also benefit from the sense of community you foster through a website message board, radio call-in show, etc.

Providing a forum or sounding board tells your fans that they are not alone. Seekers get value from contact with like-minded individuals. Your audience will be made up of people working toward a common goal. It's the perfect bonding and sharing opportunity, with you and your syndicated content acting as a big tent.

This audience thrives on more than just hard how-to content. They are also encouraged by the inspiring words you share. They appreciate a little motivation along with the information. Noble thoughts can uplift your audience, while you fill your role as a trusted coach and advisor.

Improve the World

With any sort of syndicated content you present, there's an opportunity to serve the greater good. Many wise syndicators have used their "bully pulpit" for more than personal fame and money-making. A syndicated media platform naturally lends itself to humanitarian and charitable efforts. You might assist the needy during the holiday season, or start a national foundation to help others in some way. Such an effort can affirm your connection with the audience. It gives your fans a way to directly participate and feel pride in doing so. Last but not least, doing good works can enhance your national reputation and make you feel great inside!

Chapter 7 – Working with a Network

The previous chapter explained why an audience wants your content, how you can connect with an audience, and how you can spark its growth.

Audiences are important because they drive everything in syndication. Your consumers have the final say on the value of your content, and on whether you are worthy of their loyalty. Because the audience is the driver, you'll keep growing in syndication as long as your audience keeps expanding.

You can always build an audience, in any medium, from the ground up. This grass-roots approach to syndication is a tried-and-true path for many. But it requires plenty of effort, a serious time commitment, and a firm understanding of the syndication process.

There is a faster way for you to capture a large audience, with less effort. It may also offer a quicker way to generate income from your content. This approach involves working with an existing media network. Networks are found in every syndication medium: radio, TV, newspapers, and the Web.

What's a Network?

In syndication, networks are established media access channels. They are distributors of content. Networks are typically managed by gatekeepers who have some experience in whatever medium they serve.

Once your content has been accepted by a network for mass distribution, your role in the syndication process is simplified. You can be more content-oriented and less concerned with marketing and distribution.

Ideally, your network will assume the heavy lifting part of syndication (i.e., expanding the national distribution of your content, which builds your total audience).

It's likely that your network will handle the money side of the equation, too. This means they will manage the pricing of your content in the syndication marketplace, the collection of income from your content (either through ad sales or publisher fees), and the associated paperwork. As part of this process, the network will either send a share of the income to you on a regular basis, or periodically pay you a set fee.

Now I'm not going to tell you it's a piece of cake to sign up with an established radio network, TV network, Web network, or newspaper syndicate. Most media networks are on the receiving end of a constant stream of inquiries from content creators.

Because of all the services they offer content creators, networks can't afford not to be extremely choosy about which products they accept for syndication. Nevertheless, most networks do want and need fresh content from new sources. So they search through the incoming stream of samples and/or demos they receive, looking for potential winners to sign up.

Driven by Two R's

There are two primary reasons networks want new content: ratings and revenue. Whether they define their particular audiences in terms of listeners, viewers, circulation, or Web traffic, if the numbers aren't going up, that means they're going down.

There's no standing still in the hectic world of media. You either get better or you get worse. This is the primary motivator that keeps networks constantly on the lookout for new and better content.

Like any viable business, a network or agency in media syndication depends on profits for survival. And profits are largely driven by a company's ability to grow its overall audience numbers. Since no media network operates in a vacuum, each must stay ahead of its competitors, or risk missing out on the latest hot content that comes along.

You can appreciate not wanting to be like the failed recording executive who took a pass on the Beatles, or the foolish Hollywood executive who voted thumbs down on *Star Wars*. Mistakes like these not only mean missing out on a potential goldmine; they also may spell a dead end for a decision-maker's career. The same holds true in media syndication. Nobody wants to be the one who overlooked the next Oprah Winfrey or Ryan Seacrest.

Ratings Are King

What does all this have to do with your syndicated content? More importantly, how do you get a media network interested in what you have to offer them?

No matter what form your content may take, the single best way to get a network excited about you is to bring them some ratings.

Whether your medium of choice is measured by Arbitron (radio), Nielsen (TV), Audit Bureau of Circulations (newspaper), or Web metrics and traffic (Internet), audience ratings are what count. If your content doesn't already move the ratings needle to even the slightest degree, or garner an audience of reasonable size, few networks will be interested in you.

This means that a brand-new, untested product that lacks any measurable audience may not be ready to be pitched to a network. You can certainly try convincing a network to add your unproven content, but don't be surprised if you are shot down fast. The odds are stacked against you at this stage of the game.

The obvious first step is for you to start building an audience on your own. When you can offer real proof that people like your content, you can start thinking about knocking on the doors of media networks.

There are some general exceptions to this rule, of course. And there's one giant exception that I will get to in a few moments.

Factors in Your Favor

If you are lucky enough to be a notable figure, a show-biz celebrity, or even a household name, that adds a big selling point to your presentation. Most networks will assume that a major name personality comes with a built-in audience. Star power is also a very sellable commodity in the advertising community.

Along the same line, if your content is already backed by a major sponsor or has a major brand-name tie-in, that will be a meaningful point in your favor. It tells the network that your show is already generating income. This means there may be profits for them (and for you) from day one.

Have you already established a reasonable and measurable audience in one medium, such as radio? Then it's more likely a network in a second medium, such as newspapers or TV, will be inclined to sign you up. The reason behind this should be fairly obvious. A network anticipates you'll quickly transfer a portion of your existing audience to the new medium.

How a Network Thinks

Before I get to that giant exception mentioned earlier, it's worth considering how a network reviews a content submission to determine if it may be a long-term performer for them. This will help you better understand the decision making process.

First, based on samples or demos you provide, a network executive (or committee) will make an educated guess as to your content's growth potential.

It's likely they will be seeking quality products that are different and unique, but not too different or too far outside of the box.

They will probably want to see that your content fits somewhere within their existing portfolio of products. They may also consider their past success in handling syndicated content similar to yours. They may explore whether a definable, sellable niche exists for your content. How will your style of presentation and your subject matter perform, when it comes to the all-important tasks of delivering audience and revenue?

Doing the Deal

Once a network decides to represent you, you will be asked to sign a contract that makes the network your exclusive representative in that medium. They are putting their trust in you, hoping that your content has "legs." You are also putting your trust in them, expecting that they will grow your audience and give you a reasonable income.

Based on various factors, the deal might be for a term of one, two, or up to five years. The contract will spell out what each party must do. It will describe how revenue is divided, and what happens to any ancillary and/or back-end income. The deal may also define such terms as *content ownership*, *copyright*, and *licensing*.

After you sign the agreement, the network will undertake the ongoing process of marketing your show to the industry.

For example, in the case of radio and TV syndication, a network has the laborious task of contacting hundreds of broadcast stations across the country, one by one. Typically, each station will be individually pitched to add your show to their schedule. As stations sign up, your content will be distributed to them by the network in a timely manner.

To generate income, national advertising is typically sold to sponsors and inserted into your program. This requires the trafficking and scheduling of spots, collection of affidavits of performance, invoicing of sponsors and ad agencies, and payments to you. Proper accounting, record keeping, and other paperwork must be handled. In newspaper syndication, fees are paid to the syndicate by individual papers, and a share of this income is paid to you.

The Network Investment

The network's marketing of your content should never cease, because there is almost always some "churn" in syndication—over time, various outlets may drop your product for a variety of reasons. This is why new outlets must be signed up on a regular basis to keep things growing.

All of this marketing, sales, and back-end support requires a network to invest a great deal of time and labor in every product it represents. Syndication is a tedious and costly process. If your syndicated content doesn't catch on, it won't deliver ratings or income. An unsuccessful show can cost a network a lot of money.

Now you see why networks must be choosy when adding new content. This is why you must clearly demonstrate your product's viability when you first pitch a network.

Traditional Networks

In traditional media syndication, there are the traditional networks. For example, in radio, some of the large established networks include Premiere, Cumulus Media, Dial-Global, and United Stations.

Being large, traditional operations, these networks follow a traditional business model for content syndication. Sure enough, these nets accept relatively few new shows. Their preference is for established shows with demonstrable ratings and large market penetration. Some networks may even ask you for signed endorsement letters from major industry decision-makers, which are not easy to acquire.

In short, the network requirements (existing ratings, major market clearances, and/or endorsements) may be challenging roadblocks for new content creators.

One Big Exception

We've already mentioned the option of marketing and distributing your content from the ground up, using a grass-roots approach. You keep up this effort until you reach the stage where you have audience ratings. At that point, one of the traditional networks may actually return your call and consider adding your content to their product lineup. When this finally happens, it's a day worth celebrating. You have reached a major milestone in syndication!

But there is another way to get started. This is the big exception we mentioned earlier.

In each medium of syndication—radio, TV, and so on—there are independent networks serving start-up syndicators. These companies follow a different business model than traditional networks.

Syndication Networks Corp. (SNC) is the company we founded as an independent network to serve the radio syndication industry. Let's use the example of SNC to describe the independent network process.

How the Process Works

SNC is one of radio's leading independent syndication companies. It has been in business for years and has a sizable facility that includes multiple broadcast studios in the Chicago area.

Rather than accept only proven shows with a measurable audience and major market penetration, companies such as SNC are open to the challenge of syndicating newer, start-up, or relatively unproven shows to the radio industry.

Of course, SNC and similar firms also typically syndicate proven and successful shows. For example, SNC distributes its roster of shows to nearly 2,000 radio stations across North America.

However, SNC's staffing and infrastructure were intentionally designed to have excess capacity. This allows the company to handle a reasonable number of additional syndicated shows. This extra capacity extends to marketing, as well. Our company makes hundreds of weekly calls and contacts to individual station executives. SNC also handles the distribution of national content, the sales and trafficking of commercials, plus invoicing, accounting, income payments to show hosts, and all other network services.

Since the company was designed to have extra capacity, it can capably represent not only its roster of established shows, but also a sizable number of new and unproven shows, all on an equal footing.

Unique Business Model

Here's how the business model of a company like SNC differs from that of a traditional network.

Start-up syndicators agree to pay SNC an initial monthly developmental fee. This reasonable fee allows SNC to pay the costs of the heavy lifting work of launching the new show and marketing it to the industry. This process includes many steps, such as the creation of custom marketing materials, production of a customized demo, design of online marketing, and more. Hundreds of calls are placed by staff members to radio stations each week, to sell the new show to station decision-makers. Typically, five to twelve contacts must be made over a period of time to each individual station executive, to convince them to add the new show to their station.

Reaching Critical Mass

Once a show has signed up enough stations, it achieves Critical Mass Audience, and the developmental fee is immediately discontinued. The monthly fee has served its purpose, paying the cost to establish the new show and build a reasonable audience.

From this moment forward, SNC switches to a traditional model of network syndication for the show.

The company sells national ads in the show, paying most of the revenue to the show host, while retaining a commission share. All other network services continue, including the ongoing marketing of the show to new stations, billing, trafficking, invoicing, and the rest. This is the win-win formula that has worked so well over the years for long-term clients and our company.

Independent Nets Welcome New Content

There are a number of advantages for a content creator who uses an independent network, and one primary disadvantage. The advantages include:

- Professional handling of marketing and distribution
- Ability of host to consult experts every step of the way
- Proven marketing and syndication procedures
- Established relationships with media outlets
- Industry credibility from network representation

What is the main disadvantage? It is the monthly developmental fee that must be paid to launch and syndicate the content, until it gains an audience.

A solo effort to build a mass audience, minus the support of a network, requires more time and effort on your part. Pitfalls are avoided when a network takes charge of the process.

We have used SNC as an example. But ours is not the only independent syndication network. As we've explained, there are other firms serving the needs of radio, TV, newspaper, and the Web. These companies have varied business models, but many have fee-based services to help you syndicate and monetize your content.

Each medium has specific approaches to syndication. These will be explored in greater depth in chapters ahead.

Summing Up

To recap, traditional networks have competitive pressures and revenue needs. There are bragging rights and the worry of missing out on the next big thing. Networks need so-called lead horses to inspire the rest of the team. Star power can mean millions to networks. And of course, every media network needs ratings.

Independent networks offer a viable alternative to traditional networks, along with easier acceptance. Because of the initial shared-cost model, the doors of independent networks are open much wider to new content. This path offers a proven way to build a mass audience and get advertising income.

For all these reasons and more, there's a network out there that wants what you can offer.

Chapter 8 – Understanding Local Media Outlets

So far, we've discussed the audience and the networks. Now let's talk about the points of distribution for your syndicated content. I refer to these as "local media outlets."

What exactly is a local media outlet? Very simply, it's a local radio station, a local TV station, or a local newspaper. In these traditional media, syndication is distributed to the national audience via local outlets.

Many local media outlets thrive on syndicated content, and these outlets span the nation. For example, in U.S. commercial broadcast radio there are some 9,000 24-hour local outlets, not to mention about 1,000 more daytime-only outlets.

Doubtless there are a number of media outlets that would be willing to carry the quality information and entertainment that you create.

Internet media doesn't fit the "local" concept, since the Web is available to everyone, everywhere. But rest assured, you can syndicate your creative output to dozens, hundreds, or thousands of websites, blogs, social media sites, and more. We'll cover Internet media in an upcoming chapter. This chapter focuses on traditional media syndication and how it relates to local outlets.

Points of Distribution

In radio, TV, and print, local outlets are the true go-betweens when it comes to syndication. These are the points of distribution that receive syndicated content from national networks, syndicates, and independents, and deliver it to local or regional audiences.

Broadcast networks and print syndicates need as many outlets as possible to deliver their content to audiences, far and wide. They rely on local outlets to fill this role.

As we just mentioned, there are approximately 9,000 radio stations in the U.S. licensed to be on the air 24 hours a day. That means these stations must schedule a staggering total of 78 million hours of content every year, to fill their airwaves. Syndication is the answer for many of these stations.

The Biggest Draw

Local media outlets exist to make money. For this to happen, they must attract an audience, sell the buzz, and sign up advertisers. The quality and depth of a local outlet's content help give them credibility and clout in the marketplace.

It's difficult if not impossible these days for most media outlets to create an entirely local lineup of truly compelling content. Budgets in traditional media are tighter than ever. Layoffs are common. The old talent "feeder system" that groomed upcoming personalities for the transition from small to medium to large markets is now mostly defunct. With local media outlets suffering from a lack of cash and talent, where can they turn?

The obvious answer is syndication. It provides local outlets with consistent, quality content at relatively low cost. Often the biggest draw for a local media outlet is the syndicated content they offer their audience.

Consumers may be drawn to a local radio station, TV station, or newspaper primarily because of a few specific syndicated personalities or pieces of syndicated content. This is the major reason that local media outlets want syndicated content.

Broadcast Licenses

Another reason why local media outlets want particular syndicated content is because broadcasters rely on it to help safeguard their station licenses.

For example, the FCC requires that local TV stations carry a substantial amount of weekly children's programming. Yet very few stations have the resources to create these TV shows on their own. So purchasing syndicated content is the logical choice for them.

Likewise, producing quality public affairs programming requires a commitment of resources. Rather than tie up their local staff for this work, stations let syndicators fill the need.

Large Corporations and Networks

What about the local outlets that are owned by big conglomerates? You might assume that corporate ownership reduces the chances of placing content on these outlets.

An example of a corporate-owned radio network is Premiere Networks. Premiere is owned by Clear Channel, which owns about 850 radio stations across the U.S. With all those owned stations under the corporate umbrella, why would Premiere even need to go beyond their company's stations for national distribution? Why not simply ignore any stations their parent company doesn't own, block out any outside content creators, and do business only with their corporate, co-owned stations and syndicated hosts?

The fact is, even with 850 stations in the parent company's fold, Premiere must still reach outside the company in order to grow its business.

The network must convince non-owned stations to carry its syndicated content. And it must constantly reach outside the corporate walls to find new radio shows and hosts it can syndicate. There are several reasons for this.

The Door Is Open

First, that impressive list of 850 corporate-owned radio stations gets honed down quickly when it is sliced and diced by format (talk, music, sports, and so on). Due to format exclusivity, all 850 of those stations will never be able carry all of the content offered by Premiere.

For example, a station with an urban music format won't be interested in carrying a Premiere Networks sports talk show. Likewise, a Clear Channel station with a sports talk format is not likely to air a Premiere Networks music show.

This is one reason why media behemoths like Clear Channel and Premiere must look beyond their corporate walls and reach out to the universe of all commercial stations as potential outlets.

Second, no matter how good a particular network may be at developing new shows internally, they can never have a monopoly on new ideas or hot talent.

With all due respect to large media corporations, in my experience the typical corporate culture tends to discourage real creativity. So to avoid falling behind their competition, all smart networks and stations are continually looking far and wide for new shows and future stars.

Third, despite the fact that hundreds of stations are corporately owned, most local outlets retain a reasonable level of autonomy. A local station may not wish to carry everything its corporate network offers, for various reasons. In fact, there are markets in which non-owned stations air the shows of a corporate network, while the corporate-owned stations carry content from outside syndicators.

For these three reasons, every network must sign up non-owned local outlets to air their content. If a network was limited to their owned stations, the growth potential would be sharply limited. Likewise, independent syndicators' content often runs on corporate-owned stations. I know this for a fact, because my company's independent shows air on stations owned by virtually all the major broadcast corporations.

The Upside of Corporate Consolidation

Boil all this down, and it says that you as a syndicator should not be discouraged by corporate consolidation. Consolidation may reduce the chances of local employment in traditional media—making it harder to find a job as a local DJ, a local TV news reporter, or a local columnist—because many of these positions fall by the wayside due to cost cutting.

But consolidation has actually expanded the opportunities for syndicated products at local media outlets. With smaller local budgets and staffs, stations rely more and more on syndicated products to fill their airwaves.

Local Shout-Outs

I suspect that if you gave the typical operator of a local media outlet a magic wand, they'd use it to transform a few national syndication stars into local members of their staff—minus the big salaries, of course!

Every savvy syndicator should be mindful of the importance of their local outlets. One smart idea is to periodically salute a few of your local outlets by including some shout-outs in your national content.

An even more personal approach is to hit the road and make periodic market visits. These can truly cement the relationship between you, your local affiliates, and the members of your local audience.

Some syndicators even offer local outlets customized versions of their content or advertising messages. For example, local outlets get excited when a nationally syndicated personality is willing to appear in a local commercial, plug a local advertiser, or lend their name to a local product or service.

Obviously, you must apply due diligence when you give a business your endorsement. Should an advertiser you endorse fail to deliver the goods, it will reflect poorly on you. But if you can clear that hurdle, this is one more way to be supportive of local outlets.

Super Service

Let the local outlets know that you are ready and willing to super-serve them. This will automatically set you apart from the syndicators who are too clueless to take care of their affiliates.

Your syndicated product will be more likely to pick up local outlets when you and your team offer extra levels of support beyond the content. Your support menu might include localized and customized versions of your content, periodic market visits, personalized product giveaways (such as autographed books), advertiser plugs, and more.

Loyalty Factors

How do you build your audience's loyalty and keep them coming back for more? One very direct way is to reach out and touch your consumers through the gateway of your local media outlets. This benefits you, of course, but it also helps keep the outlets happy about carrying your content.

Here's one example. You can offer to do occasional one-on-one interviews with a local paper or other local news media, in support of your outlet. You just need a news hook (i.e., a valid reason to do an interview). It need not be earthshaking, as long as it's a plausible basis for media coverage. Let's say your niche is health and it happens to be American Heart Month. You plan some special content about heart health. Presto, you have an ideal reason to seek local press coverage.

Here's another way to connect with your local audience. Provide your local outlets with ready-made, good looking advertising templates that are easily localized. These can be used to promote you to their community. For example, send all your local outlets some attractive artwork for a billboard, promoting you and them.

That might be all it takes to convince a local affiliate to buy a few highway billboards in support of you.

If you've written a book or created an information product, you can schedule a book signing or sales event at stores in your local markets. This is a great excuse for a road trip. It will give you face time with your local outlets, a chance to meet many audience members in person, and an opportunity to sell your books, all at the same time.

As you make such travel plans, consider setting aside time for a private gathering with local fans, where you might give a short talk or just meet and greet. You can plan the event to benefit a local charity or other worthy cause, with your local media outlet's support. Many syndicators have found that such simple events build goodwill in numerous communities, while solidifying their business relationship with the outlet. Sometimes these gatherings can become long-running annual events.

There are many more ways to build local interest in your content, while helping your media outlets view you as a highly valued member of their team.

Again, it's best to tell prospective media outlets from the start that you are open to doing such things. This should be part of your initial pitch to them. You don't want to over-promise, but even a single, annual commitment on your part should make local media outlets more enthusiastic about adding your content.

Owning a Franchise

You are a unique person. Your genetic makeup separates you from all others. Even if you have an identical twin, you are still special because of your individual life experiences.

Being one of a kind, you have unique talents, abilities, and ways of thinking. Herein lies a secret of syndication. If you can apply your special, unique style to the content you create, and craft a truly unique syndicated creation, your content will not be easy for someone to duplicate.

Creating something original while delivering best-in-class service to local outlets means you can truly own a franchise. So-called "franchise content" is something that local media outlets definitely crave, because it cannot be ripped off by competitors.

One-of-a-kind outstanding content differentiates one media outlet from another. It may mean the difference between local profit and loss. If you are able to deliver amazing content that is truly special and unique, you will find more local media outlets eager to join your network.

Chapter 9 – Reasons for Self-Syndication

Does the idea of being independent appeal to you? Do you like controlling your destiny, and having the satisfaction of building something from the ground up? Do you have a limited budget for syndication? Are you willing to devote more time and effort to the cause, while retaining the profits and keeping full ownership of your content?

If you answered yes to those questions, then you should give the self-syndication approach serious consideration. Self-syndication is similar to running a small business, with many of the same opportunities and risks.

Whims of the Boss

If you have ever worked at a company you didn't own (and we're guessing that includes most adults reading this), then you've had a boss.

Some people have the "joy" of working for several bosses at their place of employment. No matter how benevolent and caring your employer may be, you've likely had to bend your will to conform to their wishes. Ever heard the Golden Rule, as it applies to business?

"The one with the gold makes all the rules."

Perhaps you've had an idea you thought was worth pursuing at work, or a project you felt would pay off for the company. But your boss thought otherwise. Your opinion wasn't seen as worthy, so your idea was discarded. Or maybe the idea was accepted, but the credit didn't go to you. These are common occurrences in the business world. It's too bad, especially for young, enthusiastic workers who eventually learn to their dismay that many bosses don't see much value in bright, new ideas.

Most workers learn to deal with these slights, because a regular paycheck is necessary for survival. But eventually there comes a time when you start to feel like a small cog in a big machine. The job becomes an ordeal, as it did for me years ago in New York City. This is the sad reality for millions of Americans. They drag themselves out of bed every morning. Many face a tough daily commute. This is followed by a long day of drudgery. And it's all for the purpose of paying the bills.

And that's if they're lucky enough to have a job in the first place. In today's turbulent economy, few jobs are truly secure. Just about everyone can share a story about being fired, or knows someone who got terminated. There's no guarantee of employment when you work for somebody else.

Are You an Employee?

Unfortunately, the same thing may be true for syndicators, if their content is distributed by a traditional network or syndicate. You are a content creator, under contract to a firm. They pay you on a regular basis.

A typical deal might state that you will deliver your product to them on a timely basis and, in exchange, they will pay you a set amount, or maybe a percentage of revenue. Such agreements may also contain lots of legalese.

Here's the bottom line: If your content is distributed by a traditional network, you are essentially working for a boss. The boss may be very nice to you, and say flattering things about you and your content. But the boss holds the cards when it comes to the marketing, distribution, and revenue of your content. The boss might give your product a 110% effort, or put it on the backburner if something bigger comes along.

Depending on the fine print in your contract, the boss may even control the ownership rights and the brand name of your product.

A Desperate Voice

Here's a sad true story about a radio host, whose identity shall remain confidential.

One day, a number of years ago, we took a call out of the blue from someone we'd never spoken with before. It was a rather distraught syndicated host, who was in need of some honest advice. As we listened, the host explained that some years ago he had been the morning host at an FM music station. One daily segment the host had created began getting rave reviews from listeners. Wondering if it might have syndication potential, the host sent a sample to a large network. The network agreed to a syndication deal, and asked the host to sign their standard contract.

The show quickly proved its potential and began to catch on in many markets. Lots of music stations signed up to carry it. The host was having a ball creating the content and, best of all, ad revenue began flowing in. There was so much income, the host was able to quit the morning show gig and enjoy life as a full-time syndicated host. The show was a solid national success.

The host told us the next few years were happy ones. But just a few days ago, he said, something really bad happened.

The host got an unexpected, terse phone call from the network boss, who bluntly said the show (and the host's contract) would be canceled in 30 days. The boss explained there were "other priorities" at the network, and the show wasn't earning quite enough to justify the resources they were giving it.

The stunned host said if that was the case, he'd like to take over distribution of the show from the network. But the boss said that would not be possible, and explained why.

In effect, here's what he told the host: "We don't want you competing against us. We have a new show that's replacing yours, on the stations that now carry your show. As a reminder, our contract says we own the show, and the name of it. We'll be forced to take legal action if you try syndicating it elsewhere."

The Pink Slip

So in effect, the host was fired by the network.

In signing the network syndication agreement, the show host had given up ownership rights to the product. And the host had just been handed the inevitable pink slip.

All the years the host had invested in building the show and creating entertaining and unique content meant nothing now.

There was little we could suggest to the host, other than advise him to immediately consult a good attorney. Perhaps there was a loophole in the network deal (although I was doubtful of that).

We also encouraged the host to come up with a new and different concept for a syndicated show—and to be sure to retain 100% ownership next time!

It's All in the Fine Print

Right now you may be thinking, "If I sign with a traditional network or syndicate, I'll make certain that never happens to me."

That's all well and good. But as a beginning syndicator, you may lack the clout to demand special terms in a network agreement. You may be given a "take it or leave it" offer when it comes to signing with an established network. And, as often happens, the excitement of signing a big deal, along with the many positive verbal reassurances you'll hear, may outweigh many of your valid concerns.

Here's the truth. Carve it in stone, if you wish. The only way to have total control over your syndicated content is to have total control over all legal matters involving your content. The best way to do that is not to sign away your ownership rights, as the cancelled show host did.

This is not to say that traditional networks or syndicates are bad or unfair, or that you should not do business with them. Many are highly reputable, well-run companies that treat their partners very well. Just be aware that in some cases, their business aims and goals may not always be in alignment with yours.

Inventing the Better Mousetrap

One factor always in play is the common desire of networks and syndicates to discover the next big thing in syndication. For a content creator, this can be a double-edged sword. If you are someone trying to break in, it means that if you can catch a network executive's eye, you may get a sudden chance to make it big.

On the other hand, if you are already established with a network, there is the risk of getting pushed out or downgraded when the latest and greatest new product comes along. No organization has unlimited resources. To keep growing, they must add new winners and eliminate the underperformers. This may be of no concern to you until your content is suddenly viewed (fairly or unfairly) as underperforming!

Cost Cuts, Ratings Dips, Other Disasters

We enjoy the beach and have spent many happy hours by the ocean. Most of the time, the sea is placid and predictable, with calm waves rolling in like clockwork. But every once in a while, the ocean goes crazy. Monster storms or rogue waves hammer the coastline, wreaking havoc.

It's much the same in the media business. It may be smooth sailing for months or years. But suddenly, a corporate behemoth may slash its budget, or new research results might arrive, triggering a sea change. To avoid the chopping block, managers in such situations have to act fast. More often than not, they cut costs or tighten the roster. This is another reason why you can suddenly be cut loose, through no fault of your own.

As a media consumer, you have no doubt been on the receiving end of such changes. A show you enjoy suddenly vanishes from the airwaves. Or a column you like to read disappears. You enter a familiar Web address in your browser and get an error message: The site is no longer available.

Now imagine how the content creators behind these platforms feel when their distribution is suddenly unplugged by a big network or syndicate.

These examples may read like a horror show of syndication. Truth be told, things are rarely quite that bad. But if you're considering self-syndication, these stories might be added motivation to pursue that path.

If you have to invest months or years creating and distributing syndicated content, it only makes sense to control the ultimate destiny of that content. This means owning the copyright on the content itself, and maintaining distribution and marketing rights, in whatever way you see fit.

Note that many independent network agreements (including that of my company, Syndication Networks) specify that the copyright and ownership never leave the hands of the content creator. So there is never any doubt as to who owns a show with my company—it is always owned by the person who created it.

Fireproof

Here's another advantage if you decide to self-syndicate. You can never be fired.

Oh, you may be dropped by one or more radio or TV stations, or dumped by a few newspapers, or deleted from some websites. But typically, those outlets will represent only a fraction of your total network. You will stay happily employed with a steady income,

116

because your remaining outlets will continue distributing your content.

Unless you happen to unleash something truly horrible, akin to dropping a nuclear bomb, there's almost no chance of losing all your affiliates at the same time. Just the opposite, in fact. You will likely never lose more than a few outlets at any time.

Imagine the Space Shuttle

Does the idea of self-syndication seem intimidating? Here's one way to look at it.

We sometimes describe syndication like launching the Space Shuttle into orbit. There's considerable work in building the spacecraft, setting up the launchpad, and fueling the rocket. In fact, that's most of the work!

Assuming you've done things right, following the proven steps, you will soon be ready for blastoff.

The fuel in your rocket, in this case, is the initial funding that gets your syndication project off the ground. You will burn most of your fuel breaking free of gravity and getting into orbit.

In syndication, this equates to the time and labor that goes into your initial marketing and affiliate relations efforts. These are what lift you off the launchpad and rocket you upward towards your goal.

But once you're up there, you are suddenly free of gravity. Nothing is pulling you down. You can remain in orbit indefinitely, as long as you maintain basic quality control. It takes very little stress or strain to remain in this high position.

In the case of the Space Shuttle, it can remain high in the sky for years to come, assuming they keep a sharp eye on quality and are willing to freshen and update the technology from time to time.

The same is true with syndication. Once you have achieved critical mass audience and have a reasonable number of affiliates distributing your content, life suddenly seems pretty darn good. First, you cannot be fired from your job (see above). You have a national audience for your content. And you are positioned to earn significant revenues.

Let us consider an example. The daily radio show *The Success Journal* has been in syndication for many years. Based on its track record, it should remain strong for many years to come. Every year, we sign up new stations to carry it. Typically, we also lose a few stations, for reasons we can't control (such as format changes). There was significant effort in the initial launch of the show, and into signing up the first 50 stations. As mentioned earlier, the show became profitable after it had about 35 stations, and became even more profitable by the end of year one. And it has remained so, ever since.

Long-Range Plans

The most successful syndicators refuse to take a short-term view of their efforts. They don't waste a lot of time fussing over whether their content will reach a critical mass audience in three months, five months, or ten months. Instead, their focus is on creating the finest quality product they can—one that is built for the long run—and on consistent marketing of the show.

When asked, we recommend that a beginning syndicator create a five-year business plan. While it's tempting to limit a plan to just one year, keep in mind that time passes quickly when you are busy with a syndication project. One year can be half over before you know it.

So we suggest mapping a long-range plan, one that encompasses the long view of what you want your future to look like. Where do you want to be in five years, and how do you envision your lifestyle at that point? Though the future may seem hazy now, capture your most elaborate visions on paper and do not limit yourself in any way.

Some things to include in your plan:

- Leveraging your first syndication platform, to get on other media platforms
- Creating ancillary products (books, CDs, DVDs, live events, etc.)
- Building a business to fund your retirement
- Your living arrangements in three years, five years, and ten years
- Your ideal lifestyle and how syndication can make it happen
- Ways you can help others through your syndication efforts

If It's Going to Be, It's Up to Me

In our book *21-Day Countdown to Success* (Career Press, 1998), we included a few radio interviews with achievers. Two short comments are worth including here, because they relate to the idea of self-syndication. We believe there are long-term rewards in reaching your dreams through your own efforts, while maintaining control of your destiny.

In an exclusive interview, Microsoft founder Bill Gates shared his primary success secret:

> "I did what I enjoy doing. Because I loved it, I worked hard and got into a lot of depth, and got a lot of friends who felt the same way. So picking something that you really like, at any level of success, is the best choice."

Syndication lets you immerse yourself in whatever you most love. As mentioned in a previous chapter, you should choose a niche topic that truly sparks your interest. Once you start creating content, your enthusiasm for it will act like a powerful magnet. It will attract an audience, plus opportunities and like-minded individuals to help you reach your goals. The chance to sit down for a one-on-one interview with Gates is one example of this. If not for my syndicated show on successful entrepreneurs, it would never have happened.

In another interview, Dr. Robert H. Schuller shared the importance of following a dream:

> "You and you alone are going to decide what your future is going to be. No one else has the power to set your dreams free. If you have a dream, no matter how beautiful but impossible it may be…you are the only one who has the legal authority to write and sign the death sentence to your dream. Don't ever do that! Set your dreams free—don't sentence them to be executed by your negative, discouraging thoughts. Set them free, and let them find friends that can help the dreams come true."

Schuller was once told by a schoolteacher that he was a lousy writer. That was all it took to discourage him from a writing career. Many years later, somebody asked him to write an article, and he grudgingly agreed. The feedback was so positive that it made him realize he had put his writing dreams on hold. He soon wrote a book, which became a bestseller. He eventually wrote over 30 books!

Are you listening to doubt when it comes to the creation of quality syndicated content? It's easy to question one's abilities and resources to self-syndicate. But where there's a will, there's always a way. Read on to learn some practical steps to turn your doubt-filled dreams into rock-solid reality.

Chapter 10 – Another Path to Take

By now you realize there's more than one way to syndicate your content to a mass audience.

As we've explained, one choice is to work with a traditional network or syndication agency, and let them do the work of marketing, sales, and distribution while you focus solely on content creation. The trick here is to find a network that's interested in taking your product, because these firms always seem to be in a buyer's market.

That is to say, networks are often barraged by content creators, all of them trying to squeeze in the same door to achieve network nirvana. To be one of the chosen few the network accepts, you must stand out. Having an established audience in even a single market can make a difference here.

There's a second way to syndicate your content, which we have also explained. It is to manage the process yourself via self-syndication.

Working with an Expert

Now let's look at the benefits and drawbacks of a third approach to syndication—namely, working with a mentor or syndication expert to either give you guidance or fully manage the process for you.

The expert might handle all the tasks other than content creation. Or they might give you coaching and advice on a regular basis, while you expend the necessary effort for the work.

In the interest of full disclosure, I should point out that I am a syndication consultant (hopefully, you realized that already). Our company provides radio syndication consulting services and Web syndication services to clients that run the gamut from major networks, to veteran broadcasters, to individuals new to syndication. There are a number of firms like ours that specialize in various media. Because each medium has its own particular differences when it comes to syndication, there is no single company we are aware of that handles all media platforms under one roof.

What are the advantages of working with an experienced syndication consultant or company? Well, one key benefit is speed to market, which is achievable for a number of reasons.

Relationships Matter

In syndication, as in many other fields, it's not just what you know, it's who you know.

Relationships matter in the world of syndication. For example, when one of our experienced affiliate relations people contacts a radio station to offer them a new show, they rarely speak to a station executive they've never spoken with before. In some cases the relationships with station decision-makers go back years in time.

A reputable syndication advisor or firm should invest time each day to update their contact database. Station execs are promoted (or demoted) often, and they may move from one market to the next. Maintaining connections with all of these people is like staying in touch with every member of a large and growing family—a family of over 10,000 people of different backgrounds and interests! But it is well worth the effort to do so.

Two Scenes

To illustrate the importance of relationships in marketing a product, let's imagine the following two scenes in a grocery store.

In scene one, you enter the store for the very first time. Being new to the place, you don't know anyone there. You approach random shoppers and suggest that they buy a certain brand of cereal. How do you think they react?

No matter how smoothly you present yourself, some shoppers will simply ignore you. Others might think you're just a pushy salesman, and turn you down. A small percentage might actually try the cereal you recommend, but only if you are a very convincing salesperson.

Now imagine a second scenario. You enter the same store, but in this case you've been there many times over the years. You stroll up to an old acquaintance who is shopping there. Since they already know you, they greet you with a smile and are willing to pause and chat with you for a few minutes.

Then, you casually suggest they try a certain brand of cereal. Because you've given them good ideas in the past and the two of you have an ongoing relationship, chances are very good that the shopper will give the product a try.

Prove It to Me

When established relationships exist, it is easier to use a powerful lever known as "social proof."

Let's return to that imaginary grocery store. While chatting with your old friend about trying a certain brand of cereal, you point to another shopper, someone both of you happen to know.

"See Tom Wilson over there?" you ask. "A week ago I suggested that he try this cereal, and now he loves it. Go ahead, ask him yourself." This is social proof.

Few things are more convincing in a selling situation than valid testimonials. That's especially true when marketing to the media. Here, a domino effect comes into play. When a decision-maker learns that others in the business have taken on a product, there's added urgency for him to try it, too.

Syndication experts can often gather testimonial proof for a new product quite rapidly, by tapping into an established base of industry contacts. On the other hand, solo beginners may find the process of gathering testimonials slow going, because it usually requires some established connections. Stations may hesitate to sign up, due at least in part to a lack of social proof.

Fast Fine-Tuning

Even with a syndication coach guiding you, your product may get off track. Perhaps a similar, competitive product has suddenly entered the market, causing confusion among your prospects. Or a marketing strategy needs to be adjusted, to take advantage of new opportunities.

Whatever the reason, a syndication mentor will likely be able to suggest some proven alternatives. On the other hand, solo self-syndicators may be caught flat-footed if their plan suddenly gets thrown to the winds.

Enjoying the Ride

A significant advantage of working with a mentor or syndication expert is that they can help minimize your stress.

Having self-syndicated that first show, we learned the hard way that it can sometimes be an all-encompassing task. Not only did we have to create five new radio episodes each week, but there was also managing the marketing, distribution, and ad sales. There were many stressful days and nights.

Here's just one example. In an attempt to lighten the weekly load, at one point we tried outsourcing the distribution of my show to stations. We hired a large CD distributor to take care of duplicating and shipping my shows each week. It was a bit costly, but we figured they'd do things right. We soon found out that as one of their smallest clients, our needs often came last with them.

Once, having just left town for a long-overdue family vacation, we got a call from the distributor on a Friday evening. They had misplaced all our shows for the next week! The vacation was over before it began. That was just one example of the exasperating problems one can face trying to do it all, without solid advice.

Experts in media syndication should be capable of advising you on the best ways to outsource tasks such as marketing, distribution, and sales.

They should also be aware of highly reliable systems for content distribution, now available in all media. These include automated downloads, digital delivery, and pre-programmed satellite receivers. Software that handles automated content delivery is now popular with many local outlets.

Better Credibility

When it comes to newbie nightmares, few things are more disturbing than to finally get a media decision-maker on the phone, only to stumble because you don't speak their lingo or understand everything they ask you. These days, people have very limited patience. If a gatekeeper gets a hint you don't know what you're talking about, you're likely to hear, "Sorry, gotta go."

If a syndication expert manages your station marketing, they speak the language, and know how to smoothly get deals done on your behalf. And if there's no interest from a prospect, the expert won't burn any bridges, either.

Getting Noticed

One of the challenges of marketing to local outlets in any medium is just getting noticed in the first place. There's always going to be noise in the marketplace, which you must rise above to catch some attention. Established syndication firms can easily add your content to their existing product portfolio, and get it noticed by industry gatekeepers. Most firms also have well-trafficked websites and other platforms to get the word out to the right people.

Avoiding Pitfalls

What about the typical errors that beginning syndicators sometimes make? The good news is that syndication experts have seen just about every mistake under the sun. They are occasionally asked to "save" a project after a bad mistake occurs. One reason they are considered experts in the first place is that they've become skillful at avoiding mistakes.

There are two definitions of the word "pitfall":

1. A hidden danger or difficulty.
2. A covered pit, which is used as a trap.

Both definitions may apply when it comes to self-syndicating your content. Without any training or guidance, start-up syndicators can easily make mistakes. These goofs may be small or large.

It could be something as basic as the name you choose for your product. Unless you know the syndication history in your medium, you might randomly choose a name very similar to a past, failed product. This actually has happened. You can unknowingly begin the process of syndication with a stigma attached to your content. You may not discover it until you've invested considerable time and funds. Then, when you start contacting local outlets, you begin to hear questions like, "Is this the thing that got cancelled two years ago?"

This situation fits both definitions of a pitfall. You just found a hidden difficulty, and you have fallen into a pit of trouble.

Do you go to the expense and trouble of changing the name of your product, and backtrack all of your marketing? Or do you soldier on, correcting everyone who thinks your creation is someone else's failed product from two years ago?

If you stick with the name, at some point a lawyer may send you a letter stating that you've infringed on an existing trademark, and you now face court action or a financial settlement.

The pit just got deeper, and now it contains a snake. No offense to lawyers, of course.

Common mistakes may be the worst kind of mistakes, because of the inevitable regret that ensues. You kick yourself, wondering, "How could I have made such an obvious, dumb error?" These are the sort of blunders my company is most often asked to fix.

Early problems with syndication projects are similar to problems faced when growing trees: If the roots get tangled early on, it's very difficult to fix the problem later without harming the tree. For example, if the original business plan for a syndication project is structured improperly, over time it may cost the creator a small fortune in lost income. Assuming that signed deals are already in place with local outlets, changing the terms later may be difficult to do without having hard-earned outlets cancel on you. The growth of your syndication is stunted.

Those First Impressions

There is an old saying that syndicators should keep in mind: "Bad first impressions are hard to overcome."

A botched phone call, a badly worded sales sheet, or even a misused bit of industry lingo may not seem like a fatal error. But from your prospect's point of view, it can kill a deal. The prospect may make a snap judgment about you, one that could stick for a long time. Follow-ups may be fruitless, because a poor first impression has been made.

Wasting Precious Dollars

Most beginners have limited capital and a limited timeline to make things happen. Even a syndicator with backing from an investor will need to show they are being cost-conscious.

Mistakes can be money drains. Having to revise sales materials, redesign logos, pay for additional work on a demo, or change, update, or improve anything can cost you dough. Start out right from day one, and you will be on the most economical path to your syndication goals.

What Makes a Jet Crash?

I'm not an aviator. But those in the know will tell you that when a commercial aircraft has a fatal accident, it's rarely due to any single cause.

For example, if one engine fails, in most cases the jet will keep flying and reach its destination. Depending on the type of aircraft, it's possible the passengers won't even notice the loss of one engine.

But if an engine fails, the wings ice up, and the pilot sets the flaps the wrong way, the combination of problems may well prove deadly.

In short, multiple errors greatly increase the odds of total failure.

The same is true in syndication. One screw-up won't kill your dream. Even two or three minor errors over time probably won't harm you. But several serious mistakes all in a row can cause your syndicated product to come crashing down to Earth in a big hurry.

This is when you appreciate having a professional "pilot" guiding you on your journey, while you sit back and relax.

Finding the Right Partner

Not long ago, a number of successful syndicated show hosts were being interviewed on the topic of working with an expert or mentor.

One word we heard used repeatedly was "partner." They said the best company or consultant was one who acts as a true partner in the process. This made perfect sense to us. A true partner will always have the other person's best interests at heart.

But the expert, support firm, or coach that's right for one syndicator might be wrong for another. For example, if you plan to syndicate in radio or online, would SNC be the best partner for you? Not necessarily. We may not be the ideal choice for a number of reasons.

For one, we're not always patient with clients who constantly second-guess our advice. Sometimes, we can be blunt. And on a few occasions we have "fired" clients who were too difficult to work with, and had no regrets doing so. On this last point, we follow the advice of a top business expert, who once stated, "If a client gives you heartburn, don't take pills. Just say goodbye to the client."

As you can see, we not only dish out advice, but we also take it. Doing so has made life a lot better.

Finding the Right Expert

Whatever form your syndication takes, there is a person or firm that is the right fit for your needs. You just have to find them.

Think back to the "partner" mentioned above. We recommend you apply this filter when seeking a syndication expert, firm, or mentor. Read all their information. Examine their client testimonials. Study their business model. Ask questions. Then add it all up. Is this someone you feel would act as a partner to you? Are their goals likely to be in tandem with yours? Do you get a strong sense they would be a good steward of your vision? If not, keep looking until you find someone that fits that description.

King of the Kitchen Table

In business, you either grow or you shrink.

There's nothing wrong with hiring somebody who works from the proverbial kitchen table. But I suggest you look for indications that they don't plan to remain at that level indefinitely. If they are energetic, aggressive, and hardworking, they won't be at that kitchen table for long. Soon they'll be expanding their horizons.

Michael Dell of Dell Computers launched his company in a college dorm room. Hewlett-Packard began in tiny garage, as did Amazon.com founder Jeff Bezos. So there's nothing wrong with starting small, as long as there's a plan to grow. Heck, we started our syndication company in a cramped high-rise apartment. Today we have spacious offices and studios in the Chicago area.

On the other hand, if a prospective expert appears likely to remain King of the Kitchen Table for a long time to come, that may not be a good sign. That limited horizon may apply to your project as well, and your rate of growth may be slow.

Examine the Business Model

Some time ago, we heard about an independent syndication firm that was taking on new clients at no charge, in exchange for a larger chunk of eventual ad revenue. But later we learned the shows had been signed at no charge to pump up the image of the company.

By making the firm appear larger than it really was, their goal was to attract actual paying clients. Meanwhile, little was being done to service those "free" clients.

When something seems too good to be true, it probably is.

If your ultimate goal is to introduce yourself to others at cocktail parties by saying, "I'm syndicated!" then a free deal may be just the ticket.

But if you expect actual results, such as getting your content in front of a mass national audience and generating revenue, then serious work is involved. And that work must be done by you, by a network, by a syndication firm or an expert you hire, or by some combination of these.

Full Service vs. Information

If your budget is limited, you may not be able to afford the cost of full-service syndication (which typically includes marketing to local outlets, affiliate relations, content distribution, ad sales, payments, accounting, affidavits, and so on). You may have to do most of the heavy lifting yourself.

Approach the work with serious respect. Don't assume you can just figure it out as you go, even if you have previous media experience. You will need as much detailed information as you can find about the process.

Where do you find such information? Well, this book is one source. There are books specializing in radio syndication, print syndication, Web content syndication, and so on. Visit an online bookstore and start searching. Some books are limited in scope, others contain faulty information, a few are out of print, and some may be very hard to obtain. But if you read all the books available, you will gain some very helpful knowledge.

If radio syndication is your thing, our company offers an array of information products specific to this field. You can learn more at our online store, located at www.Syndication.net.

Smaller Steps

If you're not ready to work with a syndication firm, network, or expert, why not just stick a toe in the water? This can help you see if the temperature's right for an eventual big splash on your part.

Most experts offer coaching by phone.

If you go this route, we suggest you plan ahead. Jot down a list of specific questions about your project. You might want to ask the expert about profit and cost projections, and for time estimates to reach critical mass audience, based on your content and format.

Making a Splash

Speaking of sticking a toe in the water, here's another way to consider the choices when it comes to syndicating your content.

Imagine you need to cross a wide stream. How can you achieve this? Here are your choices:

- Jump in and swim across (self-syndication).
- Take the toll bridge (sign up with a network).
- Share the cost of bridge building, which you then own (syndication expert).
- Hop across the stream, from stone to stone (periodic coaching sessions).

These choices all have the promise of getting you to your goal, though some require more work and more time than others.

Chapter 11 – Media Comparisons

If you still haven't decided what type of syndication best fits your goals and content, this chapter may be helpful. We'll rank and qualify each medium based on a number of factors.

And if your plans are already set in place, the information here should prove useful when the time comes to extend your brand to another medium and grow your syndication empire.

Let's begin by ranking each medium on factors that might matter to you. Keep in mind that these results are qualitative on my part. They are not based on scientific research, but on my experience in media syndication. There will always be exceptions to the rule. So consider the rankings accordingly.

Easiest to Hardest

Let's first rank the media choices in terms of how challenging it is for a typical content creator to reach critical mass audience in syndication.

1. Internet
2. Radio
3. Television
4. Print (industry contraction factor*)

*Consolidation plus lower page counts make this the most challenging path today.

Greatest to Least in Influence

After successful syndication to a mass national audience, what is the level of national impact and influence a content creator should expect from each medium?

1. Television
2. Print

3. Radio
4. Internet

Fastest to Slowest

Now let's look at speed of syndication—the typical time frame required to effectively syndicate content and convert a minimal and/or a local audience into a mass national audience.

1. Internet
2. Radio
3. Television
4. Print

Most to Least

What is the potential income for a content creator who has achieved a meaningful audience in each medium?

1. Television
2. Radio
3. Internet
4. Print

As you can see, there's no clear winner overall. Each medium is unique, and each has its own strengths and weaknesses.

Radio: Lots of Slots

The radio industry has a large number of potential outlets for syndicated content. As we've previously explained, there are about 10,000 commercial radio stations in the U.S., and about 9,000 of these signals are licensed for full-time, 24-hour operation.

There are thousands more educational and non-commercial public stations, as well as satellite radio, which has close to 200 channels of content. But let's set those outlets aside for the time being.

We'll explore public radio and satellite radio in an upcoming chapter. Here we'll focus on commercial broadcast radio.

As recently as the 1970s, many commercial radio stations programmed a general mix of content. These outlets aired a variety of music shows, talk shows, sports, and entertainment, with no concerns about confusing their listeners or blurring their market image with such a content mix.

But today, nearly all stations conform to fairly rigid formats. This makes each station easier to promote to listeners and sell to advertisers. Nowadays, advertisers want to know exactly who their commercials are reaching, in terms of audience demographics and interests. Radio ratings are parsed to the nth degree.

So it's very likely that whatever your syndicated content may be, you should not expect to place it on anywhere near 9,000 stations. For example, if you do a political talk show, no classic rock stations will want to carry it. However, with nearly 500 U.S. stations broadcasting a talk format, there are plenty of outlets for talk-show syndication.

In fact, the radio industry offers many entry points for syndicated products. Stations in smaller markets are especially open to quality syndicated products, and many medium market stations are also willing to consider syndicated shows.

Major markets are naturally the toughest for placement of a syndicated show—at least until the show is fairly well established. But most major markets are surrounded by regions with suburban stations, which are more willing to consider newer shows. So it may be possible to employ a "surround and conquer" approach to break into a major market.

Radio Is Affordable

Thanks to computers and audio editing software, radio has become a fairly low-cost medium for show production. You can put the digital equivalent of an entire broadcast studio in a laptop computer. Since audio quality is critical in radio syndication, it's important to invest in a high-quality microphone. But software has replaced most of the other physical gear once required to produce top-quality radio content.

Recording a voice track on a laptop using audio software

Despite the minimal cost to produce a modern-day radio show, the old-time magic of radio has not diminished. A talented host can still use the spoken word, along with music and other audio, to weave a spell that captivates listeners. Since radio reaches over 90% of the U.S. population, it's clear that millions accept radio as a source of credible information and reliable entertainment.

Advertisers appreciate radio because of its targeted nature, its relative affordability, and its ability to get people to take action. Radio's annual share of U.S. advertising spending exceeds 15 billion dollars—or about 10% of the total pie.

Television Channels

When most people watch TV, they use a channel selector to see what's on. They may flip around the dial, not giving much thought to the source of those channels, and that's fine. But as a syndicator, you need to understand that some channels on the typical TV selector are very different from the others.

A typical television viewer can watch local broadcast stations as well as cable (or direct satellite) channels. Cable channel choices generally include basic cable and a range of premium channels.

Over-the-air (OTA) TV stations transmit their content using VHF or UHF signals. But OTA signals are not the only way to view these channels. Most cable TV subscribers also receive local broadcast channels through their wired connection.

You have to wonder how many of today's TV viewers even realize that broadcast TV and cable TV are very different animals. After all, these very different outlets appear side by side on the channel listings and in *TV Guide*. Most viewers would probably say it's all television to them, and it's all good.

A Little TV History

Several decades ago, broadcast TV (along with the major networks) had a lock on total viewing, primarily because there was nothing else available. The OTA TV share of viewing was basically 100%. Cable TV did exist in various forms as far back as the late 1940s, but wired television wasn't much of a factor with the general viewing public.

Then in the 1970s, cable began making serious inroads.

At first, the big three networks scoffed at the video rivals. They boldly predicted that network TV would easily remain dominant. After all, it had been that way since the dawn of the television age.

But year after year, cable kept eroding the network TV audiences. It was a gradual process. Eventually, the cable "upstarts" surpassed the established broadcast titans. These days, basic cable's prime-time share is around 59%, while the once-dominant TV networks have 39%.

Not that the network's 39% prime-time share is shabby, by any means. After all, that 39% is concentrated among the four top networks (CBS, NBC, ABC, and Fox). Meanwhile, basic cable's 59% share is divided among a plethora of channels. No single cable channel has anywhere near the viewer clout of one broadcast network.

Still, the growth of cable has been impressive. Who would have predicted back in the 1970s that a cable company (Comcast) would one day buy a TV network (NBC)?

In retrospect, you might say that cable won the war by following a radio strategy. By that I mean that cable channels took a niched, formatic approach—the very same path I recommend smart syndicators follow. Trying to be all things to all people is a challenge in this day and age, especially if you are just starting out.

Specific or General?

The big TV networks still try to be all things to all people. They broadcast a mix of news, drama, comedy, game shows, and other content. The same is true for most local broadcast TV stations, whether or not they have a network affiliation. They air a broad variety of content in order to serve their general audience.

But individual cable networks are programmed with the sole purpose of dominating a specific niche category.

It's now mostly forgotten that the Weather Channel was ridiculed in its early days. "Who'd watch weather all day long?" was the typical jibe. But today, the Weather Channel is the second most watched cable channel in the U.S.

Familiar niche dominators on cable include Fox and CNN (news), ESPN (sports), and Nickelodeon (kids). I'm sure you can think of many others.

OTA or Cable?

You may notice that this section repeats some points from an earlier chapter. But I consider these points important enough to be worth repeating, if TV syndication is your goal.

The primary target for your syndicated television content will be the over-the-air (OTA) local broadcast stations, not broadcast networks or cable networks.

Typically, the video networks (both OTA and cable) produce their own content, using a roster of preferred producers. The nets know what they want, and they like to order it up from established production companies. Breaking into this circle of preferred producers will be a challenge for most independent syndicators.

Also, when it comes to cable networks, there is no such thing as syndication, per se. Cable network distribution is not the same thing as syndication. This is important to understand.

For example, let's say you have an idea for a syndicated TV show about pets. You're thinking the Animal Planet cable network is the perfect place for it. You decide to pitch the cable network on the idea. But be aware: You will not be viewed as a syndicator by them. Instead, they will likely view you as an independent producer (one they've never heard of), who has a product for distribution on their cable network.

On the chance that the cable network accepts your new series, here's a typical deal they might offer you. They will pay you to produce a certain number of shows for them, under their specific input and direction. The cable network will then own the rights to those shows—lock, stock, and barrel. Again, this is because you are not seen as a syndicator, but as a producer. That's how it is in cable TV.

If your heart is really set on getting your TV show on a certain cable network, then your best bet is to seek out an established producer to facilitate the project. Ideally, the producer should be one that your desired cable network has previously worked with. Spend time watching cable networks and you may often see the same producer names in the show credits. This can give you clues as to the trusted producers who have established relationships with that network.

Best Bet for TV Syndication

So here's the bottom line. The best opportunities for placement of your syndicated TV show will be with the OTA broadcast TV stations. Just as in the radio medium, local stations are the best customers for syndicated content.

Not to worry, because OTA TV offers you a large target. There are a large number of potential affiliate stations to pursue. This list includes independent stations, network-affiliated stations, and network-owned stations. All told, the total number of TV and digital TV outlets in the U.S. exceeds 1,800.

By the way, if you sign up any network-affiliated stations to carry your syndicated TV show, be aware that your content will only air during the station's non-network hours. This is because most network agreements require the stations to relinquish a certain number of hours each day to programs from the network. So obviously, those hours will not be available for placement of your syndicated content.

Let's again consider the very lengthy channel listing that's available to typical cable subscribers. That channel list includes local broadcast channels, basic cable channels, and premium channels. You now know that not every channel will be a potential home for your syndicated show. Basic and premium cable channels do not carry syndication. But remember, you only need to be on one channel in a given market to capture viewers. Get your show into enough different markets, and the result can be an impactful national audience.

Internet Possibilities

Radio and television offer thousands of potential outlets for your show. On the other hand, the Internet can offer a million or more outlets!

The Web is wide open to all kinds of niche topics, even the most narrow and obscure. Of course, the more limited the scope of your content, the more limited your potential audience will be, in most cases.

A unique advantage of Internet syndication is that it allows for a multimedia approach. Your content can be distributed in various forms. These include the written word, audio, video, or all of the above. In this way, the Web can integrate the formats of all traditional media into one.

In traditional media, the marketing of content to each new outlet is handled by the syndicator, by the syndicator's network, or by an independent representative. But online, it's possible to harness the power of many people to distribute your content far and wide.

Online content can be distributed in multiple languages, to serve international audiences. Syndication products can be made available as free content or to paid subscribers. The Web makes it relatively easy to sell physical copies of content, as well.

There are numerous ways to generate revenue from online syndicated content. But few of these options are potentially as lucrative as traditional media syndication.

Online Networks

The Web makes it possible to create your own network affordably. This lets you distribute your content, plus the content of others, to multiple points. You can eventually own the gateway to vast amounts of content, if that is your desire.

There are also established Web networks that will add your content to their mix. Some of these networks aggregate written content; others specialize in audio content (such as Internet radio and podcasts). There are also video networks (for Internet TV and video podcasts).

Chapter 19 provides detailed information on the concept of starting your own network.

Free Internet Options

No business can last forever without income. Yet there are quite a few websites offering free content distribution. You give them the content and they distribute it at no charge.

If you choose such a free provider, be aware that you have no "skin" in the deal. In other words, the site owes you little in return. There may be a risk that your content will vanish if the free site one day disappears. Or you may suddenly find that a free site is no longer free, and you are asked to pay for continued distribution of your content.

Online Pros and Cons

Costs can be very low for Internet syndication. Quality-wise, the entry bar is also set very low. Few gatekeepers will ever tell you your content isn't good enough for the Internet. So it is up to you to consistently deliver the highest quality possible.

Another thing to be aware of is the potential for minimal results from online syndication—in terms of both income and impact. Web syndication typically pays less than radio or TV syndication, and there is a chance of scattered audience impact.

Breaking Through Online

It is undeniably true that some content websites and online creators have enjoyed explosive growth and recognition. But do the math: Your chances of achieving the same result are probably slim, since so many others are busy creating online content. On the Web, many others can easily jump in and compete against you.

Ironically, those who do break through and achieve Internet fame are often helped along by traditional media. For example, an online content syndicator might toil away for months or years in relative obscurity, gaining a relatively small but hard-core audience. Then one day, a national radio or TV show or print columnist gives their little-known site a plug, and suddenly the traffic soars into the stratosphere.

You have participated in this phenomenon, if you ever visited a website after hearing about it on radio or TV. This might tell you something else about the relative impact of online syndication versus traditional media syndication.

Note that with ANY form of syndication, you are wise to include a solid Internet presence.

We'll explore Internet syndication in depth in Chapter 15.

Ink by the Barrel

There's an old maxim that's often heard when somebody takes issue with an item in the newspaper: "Never argue with someone who buys ink by the barrel."

Of course, this refers to the power of the printed word. If something is printed in the newspaper, it's generally considered to be the final word on the topic.

Still, surveys indicate that overall, newspaper credibility has slipped in recent years. The greater variety of news sources has led some to conclude that certain papers are biased. Others point to well-publicized cases of reporter plagiarism as signs of lower quality. Drops in circulation and the shuttering of a few famous mastheads have also affected the industry's once-vaunted image.

Nevertheless, newspapers are still very much alive, and should remain so for years to come. You can give me 100 reasons why newspapers are today's media dinosaurs, but the fact remains that many newspapers still have clout. These papers continue to make an impact in their local markets.

A syndicated newspaper columnist commands the power of the press and enjoys high levels of recognition in the media universe. Many are considered top opinion leaders and leading experts in their fields, simply because their content appears in newspapers.

Many Choices in Print

There are many options for newspaper content syndication.

The downside is that the nation has a decreasing number of outlets for syndicated newspaper content. Sagging ad revenues mean newspapers have cut both the size and number of pages. This makes it more challenging than ever to get your content picked up by newspapers.

Newspaper syndication is not a direct path to wealth. A daily column might only earn a relatively small sum from each paper that carries it. If you work with a syndicate for distribution, that sum is split between you and the agency.

Nevertheless, the recognition and credibility of having your content in newspapers across the county can open doors. So while direct income may be low, indirect income can be substantial. For example, a number of columnists have lucrative book deals.

Newspaper syndication, just like radio, TV, and Internet syndication, has plusses and minuses to consider. No matter what syndication path you follow, the more you learn about the medium of your choice, the greater your chances of success will be. In the chapters ahead, we'll explore each path in more detail.

Chapter 12 – Radio Syndication: Six Steps to Success

The original version of this chapter was written in the late 1990s, when we were spending many hours each week verbalizing the information to people who called or visited us. Putting this information in writing meant more people could read and review succinct advice about radio syndication. Since it was first written, it has been revised and updated several times.

Over the years, we estimate that these six steps have been read by a countless number of people. The list has been plagiarized several times, too! (If imitation is the sincerest form of flattery, that alone should make us feel this is worthwhile information!)

So without further ado, here are the Six Steps to Successful Radio Syndication.

Step One: Create Your Show

You probably have ideas for your new show. The first thing to do is to focus and clarify those ideas.

First, what qualifies YOU to host a syndicated radio show? Are you an expert in something? Do friends say you've got the "gift of gab"? Is there a subject you feel passionate about? Do you like discussing ideas and sharing opinions with others? Do you enjoy entertaining people? If you answered yes to one or more of these questions, you can host a syndicated radio show.

There are syndicated radio shows on topics as diverse as alternative medicine, scuba diving, healthy herbs, politics, spirituality, computers and the Internet, small business, pets, law, dating, and many more. Shows on specific music genres are also popular in syndication. There are successful hosts who never hosted a radio show before getting into syndication.

What's the theme and concept of your show? Check out the competition in *The Database* on our website, www.Syndication.net. Try to find a unique niche for your show. Be as original as possible. For example, if you want to do a health talk show, decide what might make your show different from other health talk shows.

How can you best apply your special knowledge, talents, and qualities on the air? In other words, play to your strengths and decide whether your show should include guest interviews, two-way telephone talk, or something else. Will you have a co-host? Will you script everything, or host a stream-of-consciousness monologue? Will the show be funny, serious, or a little of both? And so on.

Will your show be broadcast daily or weekly? Consider your time, your resources, and your budget. A daily show will obviously require more of each than a weekly show, especially at the beginning.

Will your show be a short-feature vignette, or a program that runs one, two, or three hours—or longer? Think about your goals in doing the show, and don't assume you need to do a long show in order to achieve them. If you do decide on a long show, consider starting with just one or two hours, and build from there.

Will your show be live via satellite, pre-produced and distributed digitally, streamed on the Internet, or some combination of these? Aside from the logistics, content, and expense, this decision can affect your lifestyle. A pre-produced show makes it easy for you to work where and when you want. A live show requires you to be someplace every day or week, at a scheduled time.

However, thanks to technology, you can do a live show from just about anywhere. Internet radio is growing at exponential rates. It now reaches large audiences and commands substantial ad revenue. Our company operates a professional, high-quality Internet Talk Radio Network (TalkZone.com), which you might wish to consider if your show is talk-based.

What will you name your show? Again, search *The Database*, and also consider spending a few bucks on a copyright search (there are free websites that make this easy) to be sure your show's name isn't already in use. A common approach in syndication is to give short-feature vignettes somewhat unique names, while long talk or music shows are named for the host or hosts, as in "The Harry Smith Show." But a more creative name for a long show works well, too, as long as it explains the theme of the show to listeners.

How will you make money from your show? In addition to advertising revenue from selling commercials within your show, you'll want to explore other cash streams. You might find an affinity advertiser who wants to be an umbrella sponsor for your show and for your related activities, such as your speaking appearances.

For example, if you do a show on pets, a pet food company might want to be an affinity sponsor. You can also make money by selling past copies of your shows, by publishing a listener newsletter, by writing a book, by doing a related TV show, and so on.

Step Two: Get on the Air, Anywhere

You have to start somewhere. It's just like planting a seed in order to grow something. Your show should be on at least ONE radio station before you try syndicating it nationally.

Program directors who consider your syndicated show will naturally want to know if it has a track record. Their first question will be, "Where is the show heard—what station or stations already carry the show?"

If you answer, "We're not on anywhere. We were hoping to start with your station," the next sound you hear will be a loud click as the phone call disconnects.

So, how do you find that first station or high-quality streaming website and get your show heard by an audience? You have several choices.

"We know. He's just fixing the antenna."

One option is to buy time on your first station. There's probably a local station that will happily sell you a daily or weekly time slot. Prices are usually negotiable. You can buy an hour of weekend airtime in most medium and large markets for several hundred dollars. Top-rated stations rarely sell hours of airtime, so you should probably focus on a lesser station. Your goal is simply to get on the air, anywhere. Since you paid for the time, you own it. You can sell commercials in your show and pocket any profits.

Another option along these lines is to buy time on a pay-as-you-go radio network. You will be heard on the stations that carry the network during your time slot, and you'll be "up on the bird" so future affiliates can easily get your show.

A third option is to put your show on a professional and high-quality Internet radio network. But you'll want to avoid hosting an online radio show on a mass consumer website, a vanity talk-radio website, a personal website, or cable radio. None of these approaches has much credibility with radio executives. For example, vanity websites have amateur hosts who literally phone in their shows. Vanity sites may have a nice look, but the audio quality is low.

Here's another example: Cable radio promoters may tout all the households they reach, but ask yourself: Have you ever listened to a radio show over cable TV? Not very many people do. The bottom line is that certain venues just aren't considered professional to the radio industry.

Keep in mind that if you decide to buy your airtime, you won't have to pay for it forever. Your first station or your first high-quality Internet show is a stepping-stone toward building a list of affiliate stations that carry your show at no charge. Once you get affiliates and ad revenue, you can cut loose from the paid situation. This approach also lets you polish your skills before rolling out to broadcast stations across the country. Again, you need that first station because other stations will hesitate to pick up a syndicated show that isn't heard anywhere.

Another way to get on the air is to convince a radio station to give you a show. If you already have a show on a local station, you're ahead of the game! Just make sure the station agrees to let you syndicate your show—and is willing to say so in writing, to avoid legal hassles down the road.

If you're not working in radio, you may still be able to get a station to give you airtime. This mission requires a little time and commitment. Since radio is a people business, it helps to know someone.

Try working your way in by offering to be a guest at the local station, and make yourself available for in-studio interviews. While you're at the station, see if you can to visit with the program director. Get to know the staff. Offer to fill in for the regular on-air folks during vacation time. It never hurts to ask! Some of the biggest names in radio got started by persistently asking, and this strategy can work for you, too.

If you want to syndicate a short-feature vignette (such as a daily how-to minute), the above strategies also apply. You can buy your time to air the short feature on a station. Your local station may even agree to air your feature free of charge, if it's entertaining, informative, and saleable to advertisers. They may accept your short-form show as "interstitial" programming (meaning, it runs in between their longer shows).

Step Three: Create Marketing Materials and an Audio Demo

Radio is the "invisible" medium. Other media, such as TV, print, and the Internet, have visual aspects, but not radio. So, you may not have given much thought as to how your show will look to the outside world. We're talking about your marketing materials.

Most of the people in your audience will never get to see your face, let alone your show's marketing material. However, the PDs and GMs will want to see your marketing and a photo of you, before they put your show on the air. Since you can't travel to every station in the country, your marketing kit has to be your ambassador.

Research has shown that people gather most of their information visually. Yes, this is even true of radio managers—perhaps even more so, since they deal with so much non-visual material. It's important to make a good visual first impression with potential affiliates. Remember what your mom used to say: You never get a second chance to make a good first impression.

To put it another way, you don't want to look like an amateur. You want to make sure your marketing material looks professional. You'll need several nicely designed pages that promote your show and describe you, the host. At the very least, you need some slick looking Web pages, which can also be downloaded as PDF files.

But I strongly suggest you also consider printing hard copies of your marketing sheets, using a professional printer. This means your art, graphics, and photos must be of the highest possible resolution and quality. Rather than attempt graphic design on your own, invest in a professional designer who can create a show logo and lay out these pages for you. This is critical. You should not design this important marketing material on your home PC, unless you want to look like a rank amateur to radio-station executives.

We live in a digital world. Nowadays everyone uses the Internet to market their shows to stations. For this reason, there's no substitute for having an actual marketing kit that can be sent to station executives. When that glossy kit lands on their desk, it will say more about you and your show than any electronic file possibly can. That's why our company creates a custom, glossy color marketing kit with hard copy and a CD demo for every show we syndicate. If you decide to work with an independent syndication firm, make sure they include a high-quality marketing kit in their efforts for you, for maximum impact.

Once you have these materials, you're almost ready to send them to stations. Ideally, you will put everything in a neat folder. Forget the cheesy-looking school report folders from the discount store. Consider getting glossy, colorful sales folders with a cool logo of your show printed on the front. This doesn't have to be very expensive, if you use the right online vendor. But it adds a highly professional touch.

You should always include a high-quality photo of yourself in your marketing. You'll want a picture that you will be proud to use in your marketing—and everywhere else, too. So forget about those old snapshots. Find a talented photographer who can capture just the right image of you.

Of course, your radio station marketing MUST include a quality audio demo of your show. In our experience, the best demos are fast-paced, full of energy, and not too long. Five minutes is a good length. Even if your show is three hours long, you need a short demo that presents your best stuff. Your best bits should go at the top, because if you don't grab the ear right away, you've lost them. Many program directors will also want to hear a full hour of content, so start with the highly produced short demo and follow it with the full hour presentation.

Your marketing material should also contain a short bio about you and details about your show. You can include press clippings and testimonials, too. But be careful not to put too much in there. You don't want to lose them or confuse them with reams of reading material. A final tip: If you already have a good-looking marketing kit that you use in your business, it can probably be modified inexpensively for marketing your syndicated show.

Last but not least, create a website for your show and submit the Web address to us for a free listing in *The Database* at www.syndication.net.

Step Four: Market Your Show to Stations

Marketing's just another word for promotion, and few syndicated shows succeed without it.

If radio stations have never heard of your show, they may be reluctant to add it. Think about your own purchasing decisions. How often do you choose a product you've never heard of? People are much more comfortable buying something that is familiar to them.

You can certainly try telephoning all 10,000 commercial U.S. radio stations. You'll quickly discover how tough it is to convince program directors to add your unknown show. You can also try shipping your marketing kit and demo to every station. But that will cost you a small fortune and be very wasteful, since most stations will simply toss your valuable marketing material in the trash.

What's the answer? You must find ways to affordably market your show to the entire radio industry, on an ongoing basis. That's right: You want to get your message to all stations, not just some stations in certain formats. We believe it's important to make EVERYONE in the industry aware of your show. With the many ownership changes, format flips, and personnel moves happening in radio today, you simply cannot predict which decision-makers will be the ones to add your show. If you do things right, it can be fairly affordable to reach the entire radio universe.

This strategy is used by the most successful syndicators, and it works for you in two important ways.

First, it pre-sells all radio stations on your show, and makes you and your show familiar to them. Many stations may not be ready to add your show today. They may be considering a format change and quietly scouting around for syndicated programs. An FM music program director who suddenly gets handed the reins to a news/talk station may be on the lookout for fresh shows. Sudden changes like these happen daily, and they mean opportunities for you. If you've marketed your show well, stations will add your show because they know about it. Remember, people choose products that are familiar to them.

Second, your marketing will provide you with warm leads—radio people who are urgently seeking syndication for their station. When these people see your marketing, they'll grab the phone and ask for your demo and further details. Now your valuable marketing materials can go directly to interested decision-makers, so you get the biggest bang for the buck. If you don't keep up your marketing, you'll never hear from these active seekers and you'll miss many opportunities.

You'll also want to take steps to optimize your marketing website for the search engines, so any station executives looking online for a show like yours can easily find it.

For best results, maintain an ongoing marketing effort that targets every radio station in America. Some affordable ways are direct mail, highly targeted print, and the Web. These are the most cost-efficient, direct, and effective approaches, and they're the ones we use with our clients and our own shows.

Somebody once said, "Nothing happens until you advertise." This statement is especially true when it comes to radio syndication. Get the word out and your show will grow.

Step Five: Sign Up Stations

A syndicated show is only as good as its list of affiliates.

If your marketing has been effective, stations may be contacting you for your demo. You then follow up by phone with these warm leads.

Major market stations may be initially reluctant to sign up. They require persistence and a personal touch on your part. Your calls to larger stations might end up in voice-mail jail, but some will call you back. Be positive and friendly, but persistent. Don't be afraid to ask them to consider your show for their next opening.

Affiliate relations is by far the most difficult part of syndication. If you decide to try it on your own, be prepared for a challenge. A few may sign up without a moment's hesitation. Others will seem to take forever to decide, and just when you're about to give up on them, they'll surprise you by signing up. Still others will tell you they have absolutely no interest in your show, or refuse to take your calls.

In affiliate relations, rejection is part of the game. Logic says not every station will want your show. With 10,000 commercial stations in America, you must get past the uninterested stations and find the ones that want your show. For example, our staff places calls to literally hundreds of station executives every week. After trying several dozen calls on your own, you may decide a professional firm would get better results for you.

Here are several reasons to consider using a syndication company for your affiliate relations. First, knowing it's your show, program directors might hesitate to be candid with you. They may not feel comfortable wheeling and dealing directly with the host of the show. Second, syndication companies have extensive industry contacts and station relationships to draw upon for fast results. Third, professional syndication companies have proprietary syndication and marketing tools, developed through years of trial and error.

These factors give an established company a real edge over those who attempt affiliate relations on their own.

We advise you to shop carefully before choosing such a company. Among the limited number of independent U.S. syndication firms are some "one-man bands." What's the risk of using a one-man band? Your show may come across as small-time or unprofessional to the radio industry—and such impressions tend to be remembered by station executives.

Some syndication companies use interns or work-at-home people to call radio stations on your behalf, which can sound amateurish at best. Be sure the company has a full-time, in-house affiliate relations staff, and a toll-free number to encourage station callbacks.

Some syndication companies may insist upon owning a piece of your show before they will work with you. They will tell you this gives them an incentive, but you end up losing a valuable chunk of equity in your show, with little to show for it.

Still others may require you to sign an ironclad deal with them for affiliate relations—often for two years at a time, and up to five years. If things don't work out, you can be locked in for a long time. You should stay with a company because you want to, not because you have to!

If you do try handling station affiliate relations by yourself, make it fun. Celebrate every new station you get. Put a graph on the wall and chart your upward progress. Mail a press release when you are lucky enough to sign an important affiliate. As you keep adding stations, your show can grow into a real winner.

Step Six: Take Care of Business

Once your show is up and running, there are things to do! Commercials need to be sold, clients need to be billed, the show has to be produced and distributed, and you have to get paid. How does it all get done? You systematize it.

You want all the important things to happen automatically, without lots of time or effort on your part. You need a system to handle the sale of commercials in your show, along with invoicing, production, and distribution of the show to stations, and other tasks. This gives you the freedom to do a great show and to build more revenue streams. Of course, if you are working with a full-service company, most or all of these tasks will be taken care of for you.

Syndicated radio shows have details that must be handled for ongoing success and profits. At the beginning, you may wish to handle all of the production, sales, affiliate relations, and other details involved in your show. This is not only the most affordable approach; it also lets you learn firsthand how syndicated radio works. You can learn to handle things with the advice and information available from professionals in the business.

If you're like most syndicators, you'll eventually find that your time could be better spent on other things. For example, if your show is a recorded feature, you might want to begin by producing and distributing the shows by yourself. After a while, as your list of stations grows, these tasks will become routine. At that point, you're better off letting someone else do these things, so you can use your time more productively.

If you're smart, you will eventually systematize all routine matters of your show. Systems should take care of selling commercials, client billing, commercial affidavits, and your weekly or monthly payments. Systems can handle the production and duplication of your show, and its delivery to stations. Set up a system for ongoing marketing of your show, and for signing up new affiliates. This will free you to create more cash streams.

Once your show is underway, you'll want to expand your empire with an array of projects. Examples include writing a book, selling products, taking on paid speaking and television appearances, offering a newsletter, starting a membership website, presenting seminars, being a product spokesperson, and so on. (If you already do a few of these, be sure to tie them into your show.) Every new project will take time to set up properly. Once each is in place, you want to systematize it, so your time and effort can be focused on the next project.

Your rewards for following this strategy can be remarkable, adding up to multiple, reliable streams of income. Your income multiplies and your influence grows.

All these added ventures can help build your syndicated show through the synergy that results when individual parts add up to a greater whole. You've probably seen this same strategy used by superstar performers in other fields, such as sports, the media, and entertainment. With a successful syndicated show, you can follow the same rewarding path.

If you've followed the Six Steps to Successful Syndication, congratulations! You now know just how rewarding it can be to have your own syndicated radio show. With a nationwide audience of radio listeners, your message can reach millions. Your show can provide valuable information, entertainment, and/or resources to your listeners, while providing you with revenue and a platform on which to build a wide array of new ventures.

If you're new to radio syndication, take this formula to heart. We know it works, because we have used it successfully ourselves. It's the same strategy we encourage our clients to follow. These Six Steps to Syndication Success can help you launch and build your own syndicated radio show.

Chapter 13 – TV Syndication: The Big Picture

Radio syndication and TV syndication are similar in some ways, but there are also important differences between them. In this chapter, we'll explain the steps you should follow to successfully syndicate a television show.

Distribution Before Creation

Let's begin with one key difference between radio and TV syndication.

In radio, you typically create your marketing materials, including a show demo and a complete sample show, *before* you go to work on setting up the distribution of your show by marketing it to radio stations.

But do this in television, and you may be making a costly and time-consuming error.

In TV, you do not want to begin by creating a sample show and marketing materials, especially if this is a first-time effort for you. Rather, it's best to start by exploring your distribution options in detail. This way, when it comes to the show content and the marketing, you'll be aware of exactly what parameters you must meet to have a real chance of success with stations.

Here's the reasoning behind this recommendation.

First, the production of a broadcast-quality TV show takes far more time, effort, and money than putting together a high-quality radio show. Fine-tuning a TV show after it is "in the can" will likely prove to be difficult and expensive. You might even be forced to junk the original show and start over from scratch, rewriting the script and reshooting scenes to create an acceptable version of the show.

Why not avoid the aggravation and wasted time, not to mention the expense, and get it right the first time? Distributors have told me horror stories of TV beginners producing an entire season's worth of finished video content, only to learn that it all missed the mark when it came to the needs of the syndication marketplace.

Multitasking Mishaps

A second point applies if you plan to be the host of your show. If you're the host, you should not try to also fill the roles of producer and distributor. This is critical advice if you are a beginner, or have minimal experience in television. You are very likely to make some serious errors if you try to do everything yourself. In addition, anyone new to the industry who attempts to host, produce, and distribute a TV show all by themselves will be viewed as a rank amateur by most station executives.

Let's look at Hollywood for an illustration of what I'm talking about. There are very few in the motion picture business who have the multitasking abilities of Clint Eastwood, who can do an effective job in front of a camera as well as behind it. Keep in mind, Eastwood began his career as an actor and spent years mastering that craft. He didn't try his hand at directing until after he'd become successful as an actor and had acquired a good deal of knowledge about the movie industry in general.

There Are Always Exceptions

In TV syndication, doing it all yourself is rarely a wise choice for a beginner. Broadcast TV is not YouTube. You will most certainly need the assistance of a few industry pros to get a good start in television syndication.

There are a few exceptions to this rule, of course. If you are already a TV professional with experience at hosting or producing, then it may be possible for you to do it. But keep in mind that having one skill set doesn't necessary translate to other skills.

Wearing Many Hats

Alex Paen is the founder and president of Telco Productions, a syndication firm based in Los Angeles. Paen currently has 11 TV shows in syndication, 3 of which he hosts and produces himself.

Even with his prior successful career in television, he told me that it was initially very challenging for him to wear all three hats of host, producer, and distributor. He also found it extremely time consuming to do everything himself.

But Paen was able to make it work because he had cleverly structured his shows to make them similar in style to TV news features. Since he already had years of experience as a major market television news journalist, he was able to turn out lots of quality content for his shows on a daily basis.

Paen had another edge. Back in the 1980s, he became owner and publisher of "The Telco Report," an international TV syndication newsletter (www.telcoreport.com). He told me that running that publication opened up the business of TV syndication to him as never before, especially with regards to the buying, selling, and bartering of shows.

Find a Distributor

If you're starting out with a dream of syndicating a TV show, a good first step is to find an established distributor that understands the business.

An effective TV distributor will have contacts and a solid working knowledge of the syndication industry. These qualities are generally acquired through years of experience. If you are just starting out, you will lack such skills and contacts. It will be difficult for you to learn from your mistakes, while successfully syndicating your first TV show.

Cassie Yde is the owner of The Television Syndication Company. She says that a good first step for a syndicator is to get aligned with a company that will be your distribution partner. Once you find a distributor to work with, it's good to bounce ideas off of them before you begin production. As Yde explained, a solid distributor will have good rapport with the stations they serve:

> "[A distributor] has a relationship with the stations. The stations have faith that the distributor isn't going to send them something that is so off-the-wall or so crazy that they would never consider it."

Alex Paen echoed those comments:

> "Even if your show's great, this remains a relationship business. It's who you know. If [the distributor] has a relationship with a station, it's much better than if you're someone they don't know.

"One of the things that TV stations prize is reliability. They want to know that the syndicator will deliver, 52 weeks a year. If, after 10 weeks, the syndicator says, 'Oh, we don't have the program anymore,' it's a big headache for the station. They don't want to babysit or hear a 'woe-is-me' story from a producer or syndicator part way through a season. This is why stations like to work with established producers and distributors."

From Local to National

What if you're already doing a TV show on a local basis, and you want to take the show to a national audience? This is the same road that Oprah Winfrey followed, when she brought her Chicago-based daytime TV show to the national stage with legendary success. But she didn't achieve this all by herself.

As I've explained, it's essential for anyone new to syndication to have the assistance of one or more seasoned pros, working behind the scenes. In most cases, transitioning show content from local to national will require careful planning and skillful marketing. If you are the show host, your hands will be very full during this transition. So trying to also handle the role of producer as well as manage national distribution of your show will be far more than you can reasonably handle. The logical move is to seek out talented people who understand the TV syndication business.

In Winfrey's case, an entertainment attorney named Jeff Jacobs was the hardworking person behind the scenes who negotiated many of her network and syndication deals. He was also the point person for her movie deals and other key matters, including the establishment of Harpo Productions, Winfrey's production company.

Another Role You Can Play

Of course, you can make your mark in television syndication without being a host, a producer, or a distributor. The part you might play is executive producer. This can comprise the roles of show owner, investor, and business manager, all rolled up in one. In this scenario, you leave the details of production and distribution in the capable hands of experts, and the hosting duties to professional TV talent. You're the boss, but you'll get the best results by entrusting the details to industry pros.

Producer or Agent

I've already mentioned that a producer can help guide your show through the birthing and growth process. However, you might also access a qualified agent or entertainment attorney in the field.

Whether you decide to work with a producer, agent, or attorney, the person needs to be knowledgeable about what goes into syndicating a television show. Selecting the right person or company will be critical to your success.

As in other parts of the business world, you may find some in the TV industry who claim to be experts, but really aren't. Some might ask you to pay a consulting or start-up fee for the privilege of meeting with them. Personally, I would hesitate to pay anything for an initial interview, but that is for you to decide. In any case, it's vital that you perform due diligence in choosing a producer, agent, or entertainment attorney. Obviously, you shouldn't sign with somebody because they flatter you, tell you you've got a great idea, or drop some impressive names. You need real proof that they can help you.

You might ask questions such as these: "Have you successfully syndicated other TV shows? Do you have testimonials? Do you have a clear sense of what is currently working in syndication, and what is not?"

Closely examine the business terms of the deal they offer. Are the terms flexible, or do they insist on locking you in for a long time? Take your time in making this decision, because it's one you'll be living with for a while.

Television Distributors

If you're a regular TV viewer, you've no doubt watched many syndicated shows over the years. At the very end of these shows, you will typically see a credit that says something like, "Distributed by (company name)."

For example, "Wheel of Fortune" is currently the number one syndicated TV game show. As one might expect, there are some big names associated with this top-rated program. "Wheel of Fortune" is produced by Sony Pictures Television, and distributed domestically by CBS Television Distribution.

But when it first began decades ago, the show's creator, Merv Griffin, took on the role of executive producer. Griffin then hired an industry pro named John Rhinehart to be the new show's producer.

Next, even though Merv Griffin was a well-established TV host in his own right, he hired a professional TV talent named Chuck Woolery to be the show's host (a role now capably filled by Pat Sajak). And the rest, as they say, is television history.

All syndicated TV shows, large and small, will benefit from having both a skilled producer and a distributor doing what they do best. This applies whether you choose to be the show's host or you take a supervisory role such as executive producer.

Map Out the Marketplace

We've established the importance of working with savvy industry people in the process of TV syndication.

Let's get back to the show content itself. As I've explained, you need to get this right the first time, to maintain credibility, conserve funds, and save time. When it comes to scripting and producing your TV show, you must hit the nail squarely on the head, from the very beginning.

Maybe you think you've got some exciting ideas for a new show—unusual concepts that you've never seen before on the tube. Well, there may be a good reason you've never seen those concepts: TV stations may not want a show like that!

Or perhaps you've decided to create a TV show that's very similar to an existing, popular TV show that you admire. You may end up being told by stations, "This is just a copycat of that other show, and we don't want it."

Clearly, there's a fine line here. Your show needs to be unique, yet it must fit into an established, successful programming category and style. Too different or too similar—neither extreme is acceptable.

Some popular genres for TV syndication include how-to programs, documentaries, talk shows, game shows, and EI shows.

EI Shows

EI is an acronym for "educational and informational." It applies to children's programs. For a station to consider a syndicated EI show, the content must strictly conform to the FCC requirements for such programming.

The good news is that TV stations are required to air three hours of EI content every week. This means the door is open and the welcome mat is out, with an ongoing demand for such programs.

But your show must meet specific EI requirements, and it must target the right age group. There is a burden of proof that must be met. The written proof must demonstrate without question that the show qualifies as educational and informational content. If the program fails to qualify, the station that broadcasts it may be putting their FCC license at risk.

Who is responsible for coming up with this proof? Not the FCC and not the station.

The responsibility falls directly upon the producer and/or distributor of the show. Here is yet another reason to work with experts, and to delay any initial production of your show until qualified pros are on board to steer you in the right direction.

In the 1960s, TV sitcom character Maxwell Smart had the catchphrase, "Missed it by that much!" Those words are not what you want to hear that from a TV-station executive, when your show gets rejected on a technicality.

Cable Nets, TV Nets, and Broadcast TV

Chapter 11 explained the important differences between TV networks (including cable networks) and over-the-air (OTA) broadcast stations. At the risk of repeating myself, the target market for your syndicated show should be over-the-air broadcast stations, not the networks or cable channels.

Remember: In media syndication, a content creator places a product on a number of local outlets. This is exactly what occurs when you syndicate your show to OTA TV stations in different markets.

Networks generally purchase their content from a roster of established producers. Often they work with the same producers repeatedly. You can certainly seek out a producer who has a network affiliation, to learn if they'll produce your show with the intent of placing it on a network. Unless it's a very small network, however, your odds of success may be low.

These producers have no shortage of new show ideas. Most of them have filing cabinets stuffed with unused scripts and proposals. Nor do the networks lack ideas for new shows (what some critics might call "spinoffs").

I do not want to discourage you from pursuing your dream, if that dream is to get on a certain cable network. But the fact is, syndicated TV shows most often find national audiences and income via placement on multiple broadcast stations.

Once a well-rated network series finishes its run, it's not uncommon for it to appear on broadcast TV as a syndicated product. The owners and producers of these shows recognize the inherent value of syndication, once the content has earned all it can at the first-run network level.

Terms of the Deal

In U.S. television syndication, virtually all station contracts are written on a 52-week basis. The standard syndication season begins in September and runs through the following August. However, this does not mean you have to produce 52 episodes of your show.

On the contrary, you will need to create only 20 to 26 episodes to fulfill your deal. Years ago, the minimum requirement was 13 episodes, which meant a syndicator would repeatedly send stations re-runs. But today, a higher number of original episodes is expected from producers.

Most syndication is offered to TV stations on a barter commercial basis. The barter commercials will be the source of your income, and this can be lucrative. In the typical barter agreement, half of the commercial slots in your show will belong to you, and the rest will belong to the local station (a formula quite similar to radio syndication).

As in radio, the local TV station uses its allotment of commercial slots to sell to local advertisers. Your minutes will be sold to national advertisers, generating income for you.

Distribution vs. Syndication

As you go about syndicating your show, be careful not to overlook the rights to alternative forms of distribution. There's current demand for video content to feed new platforms, such as smartphones. But technology keeps on evolving. Some of these applications may be barely profitable now, but they could be worth a lot more in the future.

There are other platforms to consider, such as airline video, DVD sales, and digital streaming. All or some of these may represent real back-end profits. So be careful not to sign away the ancillary distribution rights to your valuable content.

Let me throw in one more option. It involves distribution without syndication. You might consider skipping the syndication process entirely and simply license your content on a paid basis—for example, to a cable network. Let's say you have created a travel show that has stunning production and beautiful photography. You could choose to license it to the Travel Channel, for example, or to a regional tourism network. Again, you must be careful not to hand over all rights to your content if you follow a licensing scheme.

The Syndication Process

The actual process of syndicating a TV show is fairly similar to that of radio.

In the early days, TV syndication was sold by sales executives who traveled from market to market, making in-person pitches to station executives.

But those days are mostly over. Today, skilled salespeople work the phones and send emails from morning until night, making repeated contacts with stations nationwide. It's challenging work and the sellers face considerable rejection. But overall, it's a very effective way to sign up stations.

As in radio, TV show demos and marketing materials are often provided to interested stations via the Internet. Smart syndicators will still offer stations hard copies, which land on an executive's desk with a convincing thump.

Industry Conventions

TV's annual conventions carry real weight when it comes to syndication (more than with radio). In television, station programmers often set up advance meetings to review promising syndicated content at such gatherings.

At the very least, TV conventions are a good way to get the word out about new syndicated products.

One of the key TV events is NATPE (National Association of Television Program Executives), held in Las Vegas. If you are new to syndication, it may be worth attending this even before you have a show to pitch. NATPE encourages participation with a separate pavilion for independent producers. There are also informative seminars to attend, and the chance to hear what industry executives have to say.

Other worthwhile events include MIPTV and MIPCOM, which are both held in Cannes, France. These events include informative seminars and the chance to rub elbows with over 10,000 industry executives from the U.S. and around the world.

Global Syndication

You may be surprised to learn that there is no such thing as TV or radio syndication outside the U.S.

It is a fact that many foreign stations want American TV content. The difference is that the U.S. syndication barter model does not apply. The vast majority of overseas stations buy content on a cash license basis.

Whatever the ups or downs of the world economy, media remains one of America's most popular exports. Stations around the globe are ready and willing to air quality U.S. TV shows.

As I've previously explained, the best way to tap into this lucrative market with your show is to plan ahead in production. Each episode should have a separate M & E (music and effects) audio track. This is created by recording the original spoken word audio separately from the background music and sound effects.

Having a separate M & E track makes it much easier for producers to dub your TV show into another language, because the music and audio effects remain intact. Far more time and expense would be required to remix a show's entire soundtrack to accommodate each different language.

Prime Time for TV Syndication

Today's technology has made TV syndication much simpler and easier than it used to be.

As I've mentioned, selling syndicated products once required sending sales teams all over the country, with reels of film for in-person presentations. Today, TV shows are pitched by phone and video demos are viewed online. A station can get a pitch and sign up for a show all in the same day, at minimal cost to the syndicator.

TV-show distribution once meant shipping cumbersome film reels or videotapes from one station to the next. Often, syndicated shows were "bicycled," meaning Station A would run Episode A this week and then forward it to Station B, which would run Episode A the following week, and so on. Panic often ensued when a station forgot to ship a tape to the next station in the rotation.

Sometimes stations would edit syndicated content to suit their timing or local audience tastes. The next station to get the reel would discover that the original episode had been chopped, so the timing was off and the show was missing a vital scene or two.

Today shows are digitally distributed to stations using proprietary equipment and the Internet, or they are sent via satellite. There are no worries about missed shipments, and no big bills for delivery. Every station gets an identical copy, so there's no chance of unexpected edits to the content.

Lastly, there's now a multitude of ways to profit from syndicated video, thanks to the Web, mobile phones, IPTV, and so much more.

So today may be the best time ever for you to get started in television syndication.

Chapter 14 – Newspaper Syndication: Press Your Advantage

You may be rolling your eyes right now, wondering why newspaper syndication even merits a discussion here in the second decade of the 21st century. After all, don't we live in a digital world now? What do printed words on dead trees have to do with modern media syndication?

Perhaps, at some point in the years ahead, newspapers will be considered a quaint relic of the past. But at the present time, newspaper content remains viable. Syndicated newspaper writers still have plenty of clout and influence. In addition, I know for a fact that people have an interest in newspaper syndication, because I am often asked about it.

So without further ado, let's explore this venerable form of syndication.

Get to Know the Niches

As in other media, executives in the newspaper business prefer syndicated content that fits into niche categories. Where in the newspaper do YOU want to be? I suggest a visit to the newsstand.

Buy all the newspapers you can lay your hands on, and flip through their pages.

Do you want to appear on the opinion page, or in the sports section? Can you see yourself contributing to the puzzle page or the comic strips? Do you hope to pen a personal advice column, a how-to piece, a hobbyist column, a daily reflection on life, or something else?

Your content needs to be different from that of all other newspaper content creators, but not too different.

Breaking In

A good way to get your feet wet is to start out small and local. That is, start by writing and contributing items to a local weekly paper, as opposed to a major daily.

Perhaps the local paper has little need for your political commentaries, your columns on backyard gardening, or whatever it is you hope to syndicate. In that case, give them what they can use. You might try writing feature stories or local news items. Perhaps you can submit a sports story or a profile of a local team. Or you might pen a thoughtful opinion piece on a controversial local issue.

You might even try your hand at drawing a single-panel cartoon. Small papers often run such cartoons on their opinion pages, especially if the image ties into a hot topic.

Depending on the work rules at the newspaper in question (and the editor's discretion), you might initially provide content in exchange for just a one-line, printed credit. Or you could request a nominal fee for items the paper uses. Your main goal at this stage is to get yourself in print, on a regular basis. You want to become established with the newspaper as a trustworthy, reliable, and talented content provider. At this stage, you're getting your foot in the door.

In a short time, the door should open wider if you consistently deliver what you promise.

Dealing with Deadlines

Newspapers run on deadlines. Once a paper goes to press, it's too late to include any additional material. So one thing you must excel at in this business is getting your stuff in on time. If the pressure of churning out prose and beating the clock on a regular basis makes you crazy, you might want to reconsider your interest in newspaper syndication. On the other hand, if you are able to plan your work and work your plan, there should be no problem meeting a consistent timeline for content delivery.

Creating Loads of Stuff

Those new to newspaper syndication sometimes think they need to produce just one painstakingly crafted masterpiece on a regular basis, in order to become better writers. Just the opposite is true, according to many professional writers. The more content you can turn out, the better you'll master the craft.

So when you're starting out, make it a point to sit down and write for at least 30 minutes to one hour per day. Produce as much content as you reasonably can. Do it over and over again, until stacks of stuff pile high around you! Well, perhaps that's too literal a description.

The point is, the more you write, the more skilled you will become as a writer. Ask for feedback from a trusted advisor on ways to improve. And encourage your editor or supervisor at the paper to give honest opinions about your work.

If no ideas come when you sit down to write, just start typing your thoughts until meaningful words and phrases begin to flow. This particular suggestion comes from a top writer who disciplined himself to turn out vast amounts of material on a regular basis. Try it for yourself.

Placing Your Content

If you have followed the local newspaper path suggested above, there will soon come a time when you will be ready to seriously pitch the editor on your idea for a regular column or feature.

Have at least three different samples of your column, printed out, to present for consideration. If you have already established yourself as someone dependable and your content sparks the editor's interest, you may well be given a chance to prove yourself in print.

From this small success, you can start building a newspaper syndication empire.

If your content is rejected, don't lose heart. You can always try again later, or simply try elsewhere. You're still ahead of the game, because your investment of time at the local paper will have given you much-needed experience in the business.

"How long has *what* been going on?"

Pitching the Syndicates

In the newspaper game, a relative handful of major syndicates dominates the trade. These include King Features Syndicate,

Tribune Media Services, Universal Press Syndicate, and a few others.

Even with recent declines in the newspaper business, these agencies still get many pitches from aspiring columnists and cartoonists. So you must stand out from the pack to be noticed. Try personalizing your pitch for the person considering it at each agency.

As with the pitch to the local newspaper editor, you should prepare several different samples of your content for a syndicate in an easy-to-read format on 8.5 x 11 inch paper. (Don't send newsprint versions of your columns.)

The length of your pieces should approximate what you see in columns of a similar genre. Make sure your name and other details appear on every sample. Then send them off to each of the syndicates, along with cover letters touting your credentials and background.

Despite the fact that millions use email, syndicates tend to prefer hard copies, not emails or PDF files of submitted material.

Until recently, there was a helpful annual trade reference guide titled *Editor and Publisher*. It is now out of print (another sign of newspaper-industry turmoil). However, copies of previous editions may be found at most major libraries. The guide contains detailed information about the various syndicates, along with the types of content they prefer for submissions.

Of course, you can always turn to the Web for facts about newspaper syndicates and how to submit content. However, most of the syndicates have done a good job of burying or hiding submission details on their sites. This is probably to discourage applications and thereby reduce the workload of unsolicited content they must review. So it might require some online detective work for you to find the facts you need to proceed.

Business Details

If you are lucky enough to be accepted by a syndicate, congratulations. This means they will now handle the work of distributing your content to newspapers nationwide. Of course, if your product doesn't catch on nationally, don't expect the agency to stick with you. But assuming your column or cartoon finds favor with papers around the nation, the task of newspaper syndication is greatly simplified for you. All you must do is reliably turn out quality content and deliver it to the syndicate on an ultra-timely basis.

Compensation from the papers will be split between you and the syndicate. Typically, you might only net $5 from each newspaper for a syndicated piece of content, once you split the fee with the syndicate. But if your column ends up in 100 papers, that will add up to a five-figure annual income. And other lucrative options can present themselves for an established syndicated columnist. Some of the obvious ones are book contracts and paid speaking engagements.

If your chosen print product is cartoons or comic strips, there's a lively online business in the licensing of such content. Sites such as CartoonStock.com (the source of the single-panel cartoons in this book) can pay you a recurring income if your creations prove popular.

Newspaper Self-Syndication

As in other forms of syndication, you can also choose to go it alone. If you follow a solo path toward newspaper fame and glory, there's more work involved. But the potential reward will be more profits for you in the end.

The process isn't far removed from radio self-syndication. You might want to review the Six Steps to Radio Syndication (Chapter 12) for details. You first must create your marketing materials and sample content.

Since you will be pitching newspaper editors who have never heard of you, you need to establish a brand persona for your content. A nice marketing kit is a plus. If possible, include some testimonials from industry people.

As previously mentioned, you should include several hard-copy samples of your best material. After submitting your material, you'll need to follow up (probably repeatedly) to get a response. Rejection is a part of the process, so expect it.

Only a small percentage of papers may agree to take your content, but the numbers will add up over time.

For example, there are currently 2,000 suburban and community newspapers in the U.S., in addition to the major daily papers. Let's say you eventually get picked up by 5% of those 2,000 papers. That's a total of 100 papers carrying your content—a fairly impressive number, by most standards!

But clearly, contacting all 2,000 papers and following up with each one will involve a real time commitment on your part.

It's best if you take a long-term view of the process, because there will always be ups and downs from day to day and week to week.

Going Solo Requires Determination

Others have forged a solo path to newspaper-syndication success. If that's your ultimate dream, there's no reason you can't try this path, too. To achieve this lofty goal, you must excel in three areas: content creation, marketing, and persistence. Don't worry if you think that you're lousy at sales, or that you have no willpower.

Do the best you can, on a daily basis. The weeks will quickly add up into months. Over time, things will start to unfold for you. This is not an overnight process, by any means.

One Man's Story of Self-Syndication

Just to lend some perspective to the process, let me briefly share our experience from the early days of self-syndicating our first radio show.

We had to create a fresh, scripted show, five days a week. In that regard, it wasn't much different from creating a daily newspaper column, except we had to write the daily script and also record a mistake-proof version of it for stations to air.

In addition, we had to pitch a certain number of new stations every day, in our commitment to market the show.

After several weeks of this, we began to wonder where we would ever find enough ideas and content for our upcoming shows (this was before the Internet was of much use).

We also began to fret about our wavering commitment to keep contacting stations, day after day. There was a fair amount of rejection, and at that early stage, only a few positive responses.

Then we began to dwell on all the shows we had yet to create for the following week, and the following month, and so on. Not to mention all the calls we still had to make, to pitch new stations!

Each day, there was growing concern about these dark thoughts. One big worry was that by creating this daily show, we had given birth to a voracious monster that would need feeding every weekday for years to come!

Each day, we forcefully pushed the negative thoughts aside and kept on. It took persistence and belief. But our dream was to be syndicated. We saw it as the ticket to personal freedom. So we weren't about to give up easily.

Strange Happenings

A few weeks after we'd starting having these serious concerns, something weird began to unfold.

It felt as though we had developed a form of radar for new ideas. Fresh new leads for content began to pop up on a regular basis. For example, we might pick up a magazine at the barber shop and spot an article with the perfect idea for my next show. Or someone would call and say a certain phrase, triggering another idea. Before long, these things were happening almost every day.

Frankly, it's doubtful that anything mystical was happening, although it would be nice to think a guardian angel was lending a hand.

Practically speaking, here's what probably occurred. Our personal conviction to forge ahead had put the subconscious mind on alert. So in the background, the mind was constantly seeking out new ideas. This helped to create a super-perception of anything in the environment that could assist the effort.

Whatever the mechanism, it kept on working. Helpful signs continued pointing in the right direction. And our marketing efforts to reach new stations continued. One by one, stations signed up.

Over time, it finally became clear that the goal was very reachable. We just needed to keep following through.

An Achievable Goal

Here's the punch line to the story. That initial lack of faith occurred almost 20 years ago, shortly after our syndicated show first began. Today, the show remains in syndication on 150 stations. If you do the math, you find there have been over 4,000 national broadcasts of the show since it began.

If you had predicted back then that 4,000 broadcasts of the show over 20-some years were going to happen, we never would have believed it. In fact, it would have been inconceivable. Yet today, it is an absolute fact.

So whether your goal is to appear in print publications, or on a network of radio or TV stations, or all over the Internet—believe that it is possible. Persist in your effort and watch it come true for you, as it did with *The Success Journal* radio show.

Chapter 15 – Internet Syndication: Spinning the Web

The Internet offers many different ways to syndicate your content. We'll explore a number of the most popular syndication approaches in this chapter. Be aware that a full discussion of each of these could fill several books! And remember that the Web is a fast-changing environment. What works well for you today might not be as effective a year from now.

If the strategies outlined in this chapter inspire you, you'll want to expand your knowledge with more resources, such as specialized books, online training courses, and expert consulting.

In a Class by Itself

The Internet is a medium like no other. Its rate of growth and adoption by new users has exceeded that of all other media in history.

According to IDC and InternetGrowthStats.com, Web usage was limited to 6 million people—0.4% of the world's population—back in December 1995.

By the end of 2012, just 15 years later, over 2 billion people were online. That's about 30% of the world's population! And the rapid growth continues.

The Web has also attracted a vast number of advertisers. Total online ad revenues reached $36 billion in 2012, according to the Interactive Advertising Bureau.

Stats and More Stats

U.S. Web statistics from InternetGrowthStats.com are a real eye-opener.

Web penetration in America is about 80%. In other words, 8 out of 10 people now use the Internet. And the U.S. growth rate for Web usage from 2000 to 2010 was nearly 150%!

Luckily for those reading this book, the predominant language used on the Web is still English for over 500 million users. Chinese content is growing fast, as Asian Web access rises, but it is now fairly easy to quickly translate Web text from one language to another.

Mobile and Other Devices

Mobile use has seen phenomenal growth. Kim Dushinski, author of *The Mobile Marketing Handbook* (CyberAge Books, 2009), says that there are now billions more mobile handsets than desktops in use worldwide. Mobile provides a portable way to access the Web and many other media, including TV and radio.

In addition to smartphones, a growing number of other devices can access the Web. A recent study by Morgan Stanley estimated the future of desktop Web access vs. non-desktop device Web access. The study projected that over 1 billion desktops will access the Web by the year 2020, while 10 billion other devices will be able to go online. And what are these other devices? Aside from phones, they include iPads, tablets, game boxes, car dashboards, household appliances, and more.

This raises an important point, one we will only touch on here. Whatever your syndicated Web content may be, it's important that you make it easily accessible to the widest number of users. The days of concerning yourself with only desktop access are reaching an end.

To serve the burgeoning mobile audience, your content must be adaptable to the various standards required for these devices. You can achieve this via mobile apps, website design changes, different stream technologies, and other means.

Local, National, Global

With the Internet, the concept of syndicating a product to a set of local media outlets does not apply, in a strict sense. This is a significant difference from traditional media.

Obviously, the geographical limits of traditional media outlets do not apply to the Web. Each traditional broadcast signal, for example, serves only one market. Thus, broadcast syndication requires multiple stations, each located in a different market, for national distribution of your content.

But Web content available in one location is generally available everywhere, worldwide, at virtually the same instant. There are exceptions to this rule, but for our purposes let's assume the same Internet content is equally accessible at all points of the compass.

This is not to say that everyone online can or will access all of that available online content. Just the opposite, in fact.

With the huge volume of stuff now available on the Web, it would be impossible for anyone to digest more than a slice of this gargantuan pie in one lifetime. As of 2012, there were 634 million websites. Even if a dedicated Web surfer were to visit 1,000 sites a day, it would take 1,700 years to visit them all. And with 20 million new sites being created annually, not even Methuselah could achieve this elusive goal.

Here is where the power of syndication comes into play, as we will explain.

Choose Your Goals

Before we study the nuts and bolts of Internet syndication, let's look at some early decisions you should make regarding your online content.

First, you must set specific goals up front, and decide what is most important for you. Are you interested in spreading a specific message, and influencing others with your thoughts and ideas? Or is financial profit your primary motive? You may desire both fame AND fortune, and both goals are achievable through syndication. But targeting one before the other will likely be easier than targeting both simultaneously.

Perhaps your goal is to have tens of thousands of people friend and follow you, and to be at the hub of a very large social media network.

Or maybe you dream of being an online journalist and reporter who informs millions and shines the light of truth on stories that matter to you.

It's possible you care less about defining your content up front, and more about reaching a mass audience, just to see where it takes you (in other words, you first discover what the people want and then give it to them).

Here's another important question to ask yourself: What form of Internet content creation is most appealing to you? The obvious choices include text, audio, and video. Within those broad categories are infinite style variations that are rarely seen in traditional media. Do you have the skills needed to create compelling content of the type you wish to syndicate? Do you need to learn how to do it, or will you outsource the task to others?

How much time and effort can you commit to your Web syndication project? Do you have the budget to hire additional content creators and online workers to assist you?

Select Your Niche

It's best to choose a niche for Internet syndication, just as with traditional media syndication. Your best chance for reaching a mass audience lies in targeting a fairly narrow segment of the billions of people who are now online. Keep in mind that with the Web, a narrow segment may still comprise a large number of people.

In fact, the Internet is the ideal medium for drilling down into a niche and laser-targeting a specific audience. You can avoid traditional media gatekeepers entirely here.

For example, in TV syndication you might create a viable show about antique collecting. But on the Web, your content can zoom in to one single aspect of this topic. You might get as specific as creating content about antique music boxes, or antique chairs, or whatever aspect is most compelling to you.

As I've mentioned before, the more specific your content, the smaller your total potential audience will be. On the other hand, the more narrow a category segment, the easier it should be to dominate that field, and be recognized as a leading expert.

Multiple Niches, One Creator

If you happen to have many interests, here's good news. With Internet syndication, you can easily target multiple niches. So you can syndicate content about antique furniture collecting while also syndicating content about breeding dogs, car repair, yoga meditation, and so on. Each additional niche will naturally demand separate distribution efforts and the additional task of ongoing content creation.

In fact, Internet syndicators who put financial goals first often do not even bother with their personal interests, when it comes to content. Their primary interest is in reaching the largest and most lucrative online segments, based upon search-engine data, in order to generate revenue through ads, clicks, or actions. They might create very narrow content on topics as specific as quieting a barking dog, losing belly fat, or whatever.

Syndication and Search Engines

The key to Internet content syndication is to get your content into as many different corners of the Web as possible, while at the same time making it very search-engine-friendly. Since only the tiniest fraction of Web users may visit any one website, your syndication strategy is to place your content on as many different sites as you can. In this way, a much wider audience will have a chance to see it.

One popular way to do this is via RSS feeds. But I'm getting ahead of myself.

First, let me explain that you want your content, and any websites on which it appears, to be well ranked with the major search providers. In this way, Web users seeking content such as yours will more easily and quickly find whatever they're looking for.

One way to improve your rank is to list yourself in one of the many online content directories. For example, search for "blog directories" to get started. Once you've created some content and posted it, submit your listing to multiple blog directories. Directory sites are indexed by search engines, and links in them to your site will help you get ranked higher.

Search engines use software robots (sometimes called "spiders"), which constantly roam the Internet. These bots scan countless numbers of websites and send what they find back to the mother ship. As the automated trackers return their massive loads of data, that info is sliced and diced by proprietary software. The results are used to update the search-engine rankings. So when a brand-new site goes online, it might be only a matter of hours or days before that site appears in the listings of Google, Yahoo, Bing, and other search engines. But your site's position in the search results may be high or low, depending on a number of factors.

In general, the more online places your content appears (including links to your site), the more favorably it will be looked upon by the search providers. Clearly, being listed in multiple directories is helpful here.

Search engines have become increasingly sophisticated in recent years. Their filtering software is constantly tweaked to lower the rankings of sites and content that provide shallow or unoriginal info, that are too advertising-oriented, or that seem to exist only to game the search system to grab traffic. On the plus side, sites that provide solid, meaty content and original, unique information tend to move higher in search-engine results, which helps them get more traffic. By consistently creating new and unique content, you will likely find yourself on the good side of the search engines.

Blogs and Article Writing

A common strategy used in Internet syndication is to create a written piece on a topic of interest and post it on a website. This type of content is commonly called a blog, although you might call it a news article, opinion piece, or whatever you prefer.

Once you have created and posted it, you can encourage other sites to post links to the page containing your content, driving traffic and readers to your site. All your previous content should remain available as well.

If copyright and site traffic concerns are not paramount, you can even offer appropriate sites the right to copy and paste your blog directly to their site.

Since many websites are constantly seeking fresh, quality content, this approach can be an effective way to distribute your message far and wide. It works especially well if the sites that post your content are popular in their own right, with decent amounts of traffic. Cultivating relationships with larger sites related to the topic of your content is a worthwhile strategy.

You may also want to syndicate your blog to online portals that accept your content. Two general sites of this type are AllTop.com and DailyBrainstorm.com.

You should also add your listing to major blog directories such as Technorati.com, BlogHints.com, and others.

There are SEO (search-engine optimization) software tools you can purchase to generate multiple backlinks for your content, which can accelerate your efforts. Alternatively, you can get a link building service to assist you. You will want to check references before hiring one of these services.

Web Feeds and RSS

Web feeds and news feeds employ a format that allows users to subscribe and receive updated content from a provider. In fact, Web feeds are sometimes called syndicated feeds or news feeds.

Did you remember to stop our news feeds while we're away?

RSS is an acronym that stands for "really simple syndication." The concept was first designed for blog distribution, and it is still widely used for this purpose.

You'll want to distribute your blog content to others using the RSS subscription model. It's as easy as using one of the many popular online blogging solutions that incorporate RSS feeds, to host and distribute your written content. Subscribers who enjoy reading what you write can sign up for more of it with just one click, instantly making you one of their favorite content providers. Then, every future blog or article you write will be automatically delivered to them. RSS really IS very simple, as its name says.

A popular way for a user to subscribe to multiple RSS feeds is to use Google Reader, which is a free service. This is a feed reader (or news reader) that frequently contacts Web servers where desired content is posted, and automatically downloads any new material.

RSS is also used for media file distribution—for example, with podcasts (see below). With RSS, you can automatically distribute your media content to your online fans. You can set up your own RSS feeds through your own website, perhaps using one of the various feed creation tools available.

An alternate format to RSS is Atom. Atom functions in a similar way to RSS, but has some technical, underlying differences. Both RSS and Atom are freely available standards.

Hosting Media Files

You can host media files on your own website, which is an ideal solution if you like having total control. Or you can use a managed or dedicated hosting service to handle the process for you.

If you use an outside service, the same rules apply as with all other forms of media syndication. Be sure to read all the contract terms carefully. Make sure you do not give up any rights or control regarding your content, by placing it in the hands of another company for distribution. Also, be sure to keep a separate backup copy of any media files you post online. While most servers are reliable, it's foolish to rely solely on them for permanent storage of your valuable content.

If you grow to the point of having a massive audience for your content, delivery will require a sizable amount of Internet bandwidth. This is especially true if your content is video.

At some point, it may be worth moving to a content distribution network (CDN). Such networks are serious content providers, built to handle large bandwidth surges with minimal latency (time delays). They do this by caching your content at large servers located at points across the nation or around the globe. In each region, content is delivered to users from the nearest server, which helps to make delivery fast and reliable. One popular and relatively affordable CDN is Amazon Cloudfront.

Multiple Site Strategies

There's no need to limit placement of your content to a single site, or to sites owned and operated by others.

You can easily create a multitude of different websites yourself, perhaps for the sole purpose of giving your content multiple points of distribution.

Those who follow this strategy can employ search-engine data when creating their various sites. This data reveals the most popular keywords that Web users enter into search engines when seeking similar content. Keyword info is readily available. For example, go to Google.com and enter "Google keyword tool." Try entering various search terms in the keyword tool, to see how high certain keywords rank.

There are a number of ways to use this information. One is to choose URLs for your new sites that incorporate popular keywords in the category. For example, let's say your content is all about carpentry. A popular related keyword entered by Web users doing "carpentry" searches is "renovation." So you might choose a URL for a new site that incorporates both of those words, such as AmazingRenovationCarpentry.com.

You can also use popular keywords related to your category in your site's meta-tags and meta-description. But be sure your site actually reflects those keywords in its content, or you'll risk a downgrade from the search engines.

Creating Different Versions

If all the articles you post on your first site are identical to those posted on your additional sites, the search engines will discount this, and you won't get optimum results. One solution to this problem is to rewrite your original articles, creating different versions for each different Web placement.

Some people have devised various shortcuts to speed this process. For example, they might use one of the free language translation websites. By translating the original article from English into Spanish, for example, and then back to English, they instantly create a similar, but different version of the original. This different version gets posted on a second website. The process is easily repeated in other languages. Next they might translate the original article into French, and back to English, resulting in a third variation in the text. Similar re-translations will provide still more versions of the original content.

Others outsource the rewrite process, using freelancers from a for-hire site such as Elance.com or Guru.com. It costs little to have a writer re-version your content, but it's helpful to screen any freelance writers you hire for their writing ability.

If you're going to hire freelancers, consider going one step further and outsource the original text creation, as well. This may cost far less than you imagine. Be sure to provide your hired writers with clear guidelines and strict deadlines. It's best if you can provide them with source content for ideas, and a specific outline of what you want them to create.

Web Groups

There are many established niche discussion groups online. These include Yahoo Groups, LinkedIn Groups, Google Groups, and Facebook Groups. Each of these services has different features.

Certain discussion groups are open to the public, while others are for members only. You should participate in group discussions that relate to your niche topic. You can also start and build your own discussion group. Creating and moderating your own group is a good way to establish an online presence related to your favorite topic.

Podcasts

We've been focused so far on written content. What if you choose to create online audio or video content? For example, let's say you host a weekly one-hour online talk show. It might simply be a monologue (if you're a good talker), or you might interview guests related to your niche topic.

Digital media files have been used online since the early days of the Web. But the popularity of Apple's iPod player led to the creation of podcasts, which are media files created by podcasters. While millions of iPod users enjoy countless podcasts, their use is by no means limited to the Apple platform. Any portable media player, laptop, computer, or smartphone is able to play podcasts.

Podcasts are audio or video files that users download or receive through an RSS feed. Once a user subscribes to your podcast, they automatically get your newest content on an ongoing basis.

The first step in the process is to create your original media content. Next, the media file must be encoded in a format that is easily distributed online. Then the podcast is placed on a server, so others can access and download it.

Once you've done these things, the final step is marketing and promoting your podcast. You need to spread the word about your content!

If you've never created a media file, try subscribing to someone else's podcast. One way to do this is to visit the Apple iTunes store at iTunes.com and sign up. Then you can access tens of thousands of free podcasts. Or you can visit another podcast database site, such as PodcastAlley.com.

When you click on a podcast link, the file downloads to your computer or other device. This might take a few moments. After it's done, click to play the file. It's that easy.

As a subscriber, each time there's a new offering available from the same provider, you'll automatically get it. If you no longer wish to receive a podcast, it's a simple matter to unsubscribe.

Once you've created your own podcast, you can add it to the Apple iTunes store. While this is free of charge, there's a short approval period for new content. Once your show is accepted, it will be available to millions of iTunes store visitors. Note that your actual media files are not hosted at iTunes. The actual files reside on your site or your designated provider's site.

Many podcasters use a Web feed management provider, such as Feedburner or Feedblitz. These services host RSS feeds, provide traffic analysis, and even give you the option to earn income from advertising. These sites will also check your feed to make sure it is properly configured.

Your podcast files should always include detailed metadata. Metadata is simply info attached to the file itself, explaining such details as the topic, the host's name, and so on. Quality metadata makes it easier for those searching for your content to find it.

Online Video Syndication

If your medium of choice is video, the Web is an ideal place to syndicate such content. A good place to start is at YouTube.com, the popular video sharing site. You can upload your videos to YouTube, assuming they are 100% original. (If your videos contain any non-original content, you risk having YouTube or another video sharing site delete them for copyright violation.)

YouTube makes it possible for others to subscribe to your videos, post comments, and add ratings. You can optimize your videos with keywords to increase views, interact with the YouTube community, and use your page to send traffic to your website.

If your videos get sufficient views, you can become a member of the YouTube Partner Program and earn revenue through ad monetization of your video content.

But YouTube isn't the only site for video syndication. There are many more, such as Vimeo.com, DailyMotion.com, and Break.com. You can upload your video to multiple sites for maximum impact.

There are also media submission sites, such as Pixelpipe.com, that let you upload your media files to a number of content sharing sites simultaneously.

Internet Radio

Another option for Internet audio content creation and distribution is joining an established Internet radio website.

But before we get into that, here's a disclaimer: When we founded TalkZone.com, a professional Internet talk radio (ITR) site established in 2007, we designed the site to provide a wide variety of high-quality talk-show content, free of charge. Content is streamed live 24/7, and there is a free on-demand library with many thousands of hours of talk shows. If you are interested in hosting your own Internet talk show, you can watch a short informational video at www.TalkZone.com/become-host.php.

Besides TalkZone, there are several other well-established ITR sites. These sites offer media content creators several key advantages over stand-alone podcast production and distribution.

First, the best of the ITR sites have the facilities and staff to support professional quality shows, including toll-free call-in lines, talented producers, and other amenities. Second, they offer live streaming of your show, plus on-demand libraries of all previous content. Third, established sites have existing, sizable audiences, so your user base won't have to start at zero—far from it, in fact.

Content Farms

Another aspect of Internet content distribution is the so-called "content farm." On content-farm sites, a seemingly endless array of articles might appear, written by a veritable army of freelancers. All the content is aggregated for visitors to read and enjoy. In effect, it's a fast, cheap form of online journalism.

But the primary reason these content farms exist is to attract massive amounts of search-engine traffic, which the sites can convert into advertising revenue. Let me give you some idea of the numbers involved: One such site, AssociatedContent.com, was recently purchased by Yahoo for a reported $90 million.

Some of these sites are said to publish as many as a million new articles every year. However, critics say the content is often poorly researched or may contain sketchy information. In addition, these sites can be vulnerable to search-engine software tweaks, which can suddenly downgrade their search rankings.

Partial vs. Full Content Syndication

When it comes to RSS feeds of your content, there's an option to consider: the choice between "partial" and "full" content syndication. This is simpler than it may sound. Partial content syndication simply means you distribute only a mini-version of your content to subscribers—what one might call a teaser or abridged version. If someone is intrigued by the teaser, they must click over to your site for the complete piece.

As you probably realize, full content syndication is just the opposite—subscribers get the whole enchilada in the download.

There are pluses and minuses to each approach. Partial syndication may save you bandwidth, and save your subscribers time. They get a quick thumbnail of your content. If they're not interested in it, there's no need for them to download the full version. On the other hand, some subscribers might not be happy about the extra step required to get your full content. Basic inertia might cause others to always skip the full download, so they never bother getting all of the content you worked so hard to create.

There may be some who never subscribe to your content in the first place, if they see that you limit the subscription to partial content. These folks want it all—or nothing at all.

Given a choice, my preference would be full content syndication, but the decision is up to you.

Licensing Your Content

We touched on this idea earlier: syndicating your quality content to multiple websites owned by others. In exchange, these sites might be willing to pay you a licensing fee.

In order for a business arrangement like this to work for both parties, the content you provide must be fresh and unique. Obviously, no one will pay you for stale stuff that can be found elsewhere. You must also be willing to deliver the content on a consistent basis and meet promised deadlines.

There are a number of major, established content licensing sites that provide this type of service. These firms deliver news-headline feeds, weather feeds, stock info, and other timely products to thousands of websites. These providers help the subscribing sites appear fresh and up-to-date, while giving visitors new content to absorb each time they visit.

One such syndicator is CNN RSS, which licenses an RSS feed of CNN content to sites. Others include Associated Press and ESPN. News aggregators such as Feedzilla combine a number of services in their offering, giving subscribers a whole menu of options.

If you decide to toss your hat into this ring, understand that you will face competition from the large, established content licensing sites. Your best bet will be to focus your licensed content in a tight niche, and then target subscribing sites that are in the same niche category. Don't expect to charge huge fees for your content, either. Some providers license their content for just a few dollars a month. Your specific niche, and the level of demand you get for your content, will help you determine the right fee to charge.

In Chapter 17, we'll further explore revenue generation from syndicated Web content.

Using Widgets

Another way to syndicate your content to other sites is to create an attractive widget. A well-designed Web widget offers sites a neat way to provide fresh content. Many widgets automatically update themselves, with no effort on the part of the subscribing site. Content on a widget can attract a great deal of interest and plenty of clickthrough traffic to the creator's website.

Many sites are willing to give up the "real estate" to find room for a widget, if it provides worthwhile content and attracts site-visitor interest. Sometimes just adding a popular widget can boost site traffic.

You can create your own Web widget at sites such as iwidget.com and widgadget.com. Widget-creation sites let you to customize the type of widget you want, the color, layout, and other elements. A typical widget might offer a daily poll on a hot topic, and a link to view the poll results or to visit the source website.

There are also desktop widgets that users can install on their computer, and mobile widgets for installation on mobile devices.

Viral Syndication

In most forms of content syndication, the creator (you or someone you hire) has to do the heavy lifting work of distributing your content to as many outlets as possible. It takes time and persistent effort.

But the Internet offers a tantalizing way to let the audience do all the work, with results that go beyond your wildest imagination.

Let's say you created a "vblog" (video blog) that profiles a fascinating but little-known personality. You post the video online and it attracts a modest level of interest. A few days later, a major news story breaks involving this same obscure personality. Suddenly, thousands of people rush to the Web to learn more about the elusive figure. The search engines contain only one link with meaningful info. It happens to be the video you created!

Your video viewership suddenly surges. Within minutes, thousands more turn to Facebook, Twitter, mobile texts and email, urging friends and family to watch the video. Direct links to your video are quickly posted on hundreds of other sites. Within a short time, thousands of views turn into 100 thousand views. Viewership explodes. Your video has just gone viral, and could soon have millions of views. And the crazy thing is, you had nothing to do with it.

If viral syndication happens to you, it can be a blessing or a curse, and sometimes both. The blessing can be immediate worldwide fame for you and your content. All the struggles you've endured to find recognition are suddenly over. Instantly, you become a household name.

Some possible downsides? If the viral content somehow has a negative tilt or puts you in a bad light, it can mean trouble. For example, imagine someone posts a video of you kicking your dog. If it goes viral, it might result in an endless barrage of hate email and outrage from countless numbers of animal lovers. In almost no time, your formerly good name will turn to mud, all across the nation (and some might say you deserve it for booting that poor pooch).

Even if the viral result isn't quite this awful, the actual outcome may be hard to control.

Let's say that, for some other reason, people rush en masse to learn more about you, the clever content creator. But the only image of you in the search engines is a very old, goofy-looking snapshot, posted months ago to a social media site. Since first impressions tend to stick, everyone around the country now believes that's an accurate photo of you, and that you look like a total dork.

Another frustrating scenario might be technical in nature. For example, an amazing video you created suddenly goes viral, but your economy-priced website can't handle the traffic and it crashes within minutes. However, some clever person manages to snag a copy of your video before your site goes down. He quickly posts it on his robust site and gets millions of clicks. He also profits handsomely by inserting a pre-roll video ad, which plays just before your video. Meanwhile, you're left with nothing but a broken website.

Controlled Syndication

A far better way to handle viral syndication is to plan for it. This might be called controlled syndication.

For example, even if you can't afford to post all your content on a server with massive capacity, you can set up an account at a big CDN, such as Amazon Cloudfront, at no cost. You can then set up a redirect from your site to the high-capacity CDN, should traffic suddenly spike.

In controlled syndication, you also take steps to limit outright theft of your content, by making it hard to copy or embed. You might consider branding your content—for example, by adding a watermark, logo bug, or even a small copyright notice in one corner of your videos.

Another idea is to periodically search the Web to see what information and images of yourself and your content are out there. That way, you're at least prepared to counter something unpleasant if it should explode virally. You might also discover that there are unauthorized users of your content, an unfortunate, all-too-common scenario when it comes to Web syndication.

Social Websites

No review of Internet syndication is complete without a discussion of social websites and services. There are now hundreds of social networking and bookmarking sites and services worldwide, in dozens of languages.

One of the best known social media sites is Facebook, which reportedly now has one billion users. Here you can create a profile, add personal details, images, and links. It is relatively easy to post your syndicated content (blog or media file) on your Facebook page, so others can see and share it. You can also create a Facebook Fan Page to communicate with your fans and share news and information in a social manner.

For example, the aforementioned TalkZone.com has a popular Facebook page at facebook.com/TalkZone.

Google+ is one of the fastest-growing social media sites ever, and is designed for easy content sharing among its users. It smoothly integrates with YouTube and other Google media platforms. It allows real-time multimedia sharing and streaming, ideal for getting others to discover and share your syndicated content.

Twitter is a highly popular microblogging service.

A Twitter post is limited to 140 characters. Still, this can be a good way to alert others of new content availability or to simply provide short, headline-type insights and comments. For example, posts are added to my own Twitter page (twitter.com/witting) regularly. Many of the posts contain links to radio- or syndication-related content.

If you wish to tap the full potential of social media sites, you must remain active and involved with them, and this can take time.

There are social bookmarking sites as well. These include Reddit.com, Delicious.com, Digg.com, StumbleUpon.com, and others. Sites like these allow users to share, save, and find bookmarks of interest, and in some cases interact socially. Of special interest to us here is that these sites are ideal for helping people find content and recommend it to many others. There can be a viral effect, where your blog or other content is suddenly mentioned on multiple social networks, discussion forums, and other online gathering places. Should your content manage to land on the front page of one of the social bookmarking sites, you will see powerful things happen.

Each site has a unique community of users, and each offers users various features. For example, Reddit.com has what are called subreddits, which are specialized topic pages. There may be a topic-appropriate place here to offer your content to interested users.

Most of these sites have "power users," people who are influencers with added clout and control. As in any social community, becoming a powerful figure requires an investment of time and effort. After familiarizing yourself with these sites, you might want to choose one or more sites in which to concentrate your efforts to become more influential over time. But your ability to attract large amounts of traffic and affect the discussion will be limited until you become more established.

Social blogmarking sites, otherwise known as blog bookmarking sites, are another variation of social sites. Here, users can suggest blogs and vote on them. With their more democratic approach, the need to become a power user is not a factor. Yet a blog can get plenty of traffic if it gets enough votes on one of these sites. Some examples of blogmarking sites are blogengage.com and blokube.com.

Lastly, there are social bookmarking and sharing widgets that are easy to add to your site. These include Share This, Add This, and Add to Any. Rather than including multiple links to a number of social sites, you can offer your visitors many ways to share content via a single, tiny, all-in-one widget.

Synchronous Tools

The digital world has a number of communication channels that operate in virtual real time. These include mobile texts, instant messages, web seminars, video conferences, and more. These technologies enable you to be in touch with your "tribe" on an immediate, live basis. There can be back-and-forth communication as well, giving you immediate feedback similar to a live, in-person audience.

Connecting on the Web

As you have probably concluded, the easiest part of Internet syndication is the content distribution. Just about anyone can upload their content to the Web and make it available to millions. The real challenge to Web syndication is in spreading the word to people that your content exists, and motivating them to actually sample it. Once that happens, it's up to you and the quality of your product to keep them interested and involved.

Mastering as many online communication channels as possible, including blogging, social media, RSS feeds, Web groups, widgets, and more will help you become a master of Internet syndication.

Chapter 16 – More Media Choices

So far we've discussed domestic commercial radio syndication, domestic commercial television syndication, newspaper syndication, and Web syndication. But there are other ways to syndicate and distribute your content. We'll explore some of those possibilities here.

This isn't meant to be the sum total of all media syndication opportunities. But these are the alternative paths I'm most often asked about.

Public Radio

To get some answers about public radio syndication, I spoke with Eric Nuzum, VP of programming at National Public Radio (NPR), who said the following:

> "There are 350 programs available to public radio stations. Seventeen of those programs account for half of all public radio listening, nationally. All the rest are vying for space. So we tend to not add things unless we're sure there's a reason [that show] should be the 351st."

Submission of content to NPR requires completion of a legal release form, and you may also be told that your chances are minimal. In explaining the criteria for acceptance, Nuzum said, "There's a lot of stuff...that we cover. What are they doing that is additive to the things that we already offer?"

If your show already has a track record of success on a local public station, NPR acceptance is much more likely. However, Nuzum did say that there have been a few instances where the network picked up a show that lacked any history of local popularity.

NPR staff produces eight shows. Another seventeen shows come from outside producers and are distributed by the network. Local public stations pick and choose from an a la carte menu, which includes popular offerings such as "Morning Edition," "Car Talk," and "Fresh Air." Other public networks produce a raft of shows that stations can choose from, as well.

In return, stations pay the network on a per-program basis. In the case of NPR's popular news content, fees are based upon the station's audience size. For other shows, the payment formula relies on total station revenue. Other public radio networks operate in much the same manner. Payments for content flow from the stations to the networks, and then to the outside producers.

Nuzum said that most local public stations accept content submissions from outside producers. This path likely offers the best bet for breaking into public radio with your syndicated show.

As in commercial radio syndication, one way to get started is to get your show heard on a single public station—on a free basis, if necessary. Then, begin building your station list by signing up additional stations. At some point you may decide to pitch a network, such as NPR, to handle the distribution of your show. Or you can just stick with independent distribution, as many others have.

Here's something to be aware of as you grow nationally. NPR will lease time on their satellite to any outside producer. So if your show needs satellite distribution (for example, if it is fed live), this platform might provide some added credibility as you sign up public stations to carry your show.

Public Television

Perhaps you have a television show you'd like to syndicate to Public TV. One thing to be aware of is that, unlike the NPR radio network, PBS (Public Broadcasting Service) does not produce any of its own content. All the shows come from outside producers. The role of PBS is to distribute those shows to its member stations.

PBS is the largest public TV network, but there are others—such as American Public Television and NETA.

If you wish to submit a finished DVD of your TV show for consideration by PBS, you can find full submission details on their website (www.pbs.org). The site includes a downloadable release form and a checklist. If your show is only in the idea stage, you will have to complete a fairly complex written proposal, including a business plan that lays out your funding resources. The network schedules its programming up to a full year in advance, so the approval process may be lengthy.

As a member station of PBS, a local outlet can carry some or all of the network shows. But a typical PBS station will also air a good deal of content from third-party networks and producers.

Like public radio stations, all public TV stations are allowed to pick and choose the outside shows they wish to air. The stations then pay fees to the networks and producers, based upon which shows they carry.

This menu-driven system explains why the program schedule of a public TV station in one city will vary so much from the program lineup in another city. However, this open scheduling system can provide you with greater opportunities as an independent content provider. Since stations are not forced to air long, continuous blocks of network shows (as in commercial TV), each outlet has the option of running an outside show whenever they wish. The next show they add to their schedule could be yours!

Public TV Payments

Local public stations typically raise annual operating funds through a combination of corporate donations and audience contributions. A large percentage of income goes toward the programming budget. Out of this budget, each local outlet pays its outside program producers.

If your show is accepted for distribution by one of the public TV networks, they will not only manage the distribution of the show for you; they will also collect payments from each individual station and remit payment to you. All you have to do is deliver your content in a timely and professional way to the network. How much you are paid will depend on whatever terms you have negotiated with the public network.

Of course, you can also self-syndicate your content to public TV stations on a fee basis.

Due to public TV's reliance on cash budgets for program content, there may be a longer approval process for your content than you might experience in commercial TV. For example, if funds are tight at a local outlet, your show may have to sit on the sidelines until next year's budget is implemented. Then, once your show is included in the list of approved expenditures, it will appear on the station's programming schedule.

Satellite Radio

During the 1990s, satellite radio became a viable force in the U.S. media landscape. Originally, there were two competing satellite systems: XM and Sirius. Each of these firms used different satellite systems to transmit multiple channels of audio content to consumers, who paid a monthly fee to receive the signals via proprietary receivers.

Despite the fact that the two services were always meant to be competitors, the government eventually permitted them to merge into one entity, now known as SiriusXM Satellite Radio. The merged company continues to offer a wide mix of content, including a variety of talk shows and music shows covering nearly every programming genre.

Jeremy Coleman is SVP for talk and entertainment programming at SiriusXM Radio. He oversees the news programming, as well as the programming for the talk and other non-music, non-sports entertainment satellite channels.

He told us that SiriusXM does carry a small number of select syndicated talk shows. And he said that his company does accept proposals to add syndicated shows. He explained the straightforward submission process.

To submit a talk show to SiriusXM, send a description and sample show to Talk Programming, SiriusXM, 1221 Avenue of the Americas, New York, NY 10020. Your show will then be reviewed by a team of producers.

Should you wish to submit a show in a different genre, such as music or sports, your best bet is to add the type of programming in the above shipping address (e.g., Music Programming, Sports Programming, Religious Programming, etc.). Then the proper department will receive your submission for review.

As you might expect, the satellite radio company receives many such proposals. For this reason, you should expect that you will get a response only if they have a specific interest in your show.

When we asked Coleman what makes his team take one show over another, this was his exact response: "Generally, the syndicated shows we carry tend to be the most popular or the most unique."

Our interpretation: If your show already has an audience on broadcast radio, that will put you ahead of the pack in getting on satellite radio.

As to the business arrangements for satellite syndication, the company generally works with barter terms (see Chapter 17 for more on barter). But the company is also known to pay for premium content. And they have reportedly also accepted payment for clearance of certain shows (otherwise known as "brokered time"), but this is likely rare. If you hope to buy time on SiriusXM, you will probably do best if your show is a short-form product (for example, 60 or 90 seconds in length), which can be run in commercial slots.

In most cases, the primary factor for acceptance of any syndicated show by SiriusXM is how much they think it will please their audience of paid subscribers. It's easy to see why this may be the case. A glance at the company's published income statement shows that the majority of revenue is derived from subscriptions, while a much smaller share is from advertising sales.

International Syndication

If you're ready to reach out to the entire world, international syndication may be the answer to your dreams. For the sake of the discussion, we'll assume that your content originates in the United States. But if you live in another country, many of the same rules will still apply for international distribution.

Why would a U.S. producer consider global distribution, when their syndicated product is in the English language and was specifically created to serve American consumers?

As we've already stated, one of America's most popular exports is media. Watch the tube in most foreign countries, and you'll see U.S. produced TV shows popping up all over the place. For example, reruns of the original "Star Trek" series now air in 75 countries around the globe.

The same interest in American media holds true for radio. Listen to certain stations in overseas markets, and you're likely to hear syndicated radio content that originated in the U.S. This is especially true with music-based formats, which makes sense considering the global followings of many U.S. pop and rock acts.

What about newspapers? A number of foreign newspapers run syndicated columnists and other content that was created in the states.

In general, the potential overseas market isn't as broad as the American market in terms of content. But there are still opportunities to place lots of content in other countries.

If your product is very U.S.-centric, such as a talk show about domestic politics, it may not do well outside our borders. Still, other types of syndicated content do garner foreign interest.

Cash for Content

Strictly speaking, there is really very little syndication of media in other countries. The concept of syndication is uniquely American. Most of what happens overseas is not syndication per se, but the licensing of content on a cash basis. This also means foreign barter advertising is rarely seen. Despite the inaccuracy in calling it syndication, most people in the business still refer to what we're discussing here as international syndication, so we will, too. Just be aware that if a foreign outlet is interested in your content, it is probably expecting to license it for a fee.

If you work with an established syndication firm, network, or agency, they may tap into the foreign market on your behalf. As always, you should closely review the terms of your deal to ensure you are paid for any overseas licensing fees your content generates.

If you self-syndicate, there's no reason you can't try to license your content to overseas outlets. It's difficult to get rich doing this, but it can provide extra cash income. Billing and payment may be as easy as setting up a PayPal account. And of course, content distribution to any worldwide location is now a simple matter, thanks to the Internet.

Language Barrier

As explained in Chapter 13, if you're creating syndicated TV content and have even an inkling that it might one day play in an overseas market, it's vital that you create a separate audio track containing the music and sound effects, called an M & E (music and effects) track. Do this in the original production process, and foreign language dubbing of your show will be far faster, easier, and cheaper. There will be no need to reconstruct the entire soundtrack from scratch, when versions in different languages are required.

Of course, dubbing a show with onscreen actors involves time and expense. First, a foreign language script writer must translate the

English dialogue into the desired language. The script must also be adapted, so the foreign dialogue will closely fit the mouth movements of the video performers. A cast of voice actors must record the new dialogue. Lastly, the spoken audio must be edited and mixed to create a final soundtrack. There are a number of companies that handle all these steps as a turnkey service.

Certain countries or regions may prefer getting subtitled versions of U.S. TV shows, with the original English language soundtrack intact. That way, the same show can be enjoyed by both native-speaking and English-speaking viewers.

What about radio? In that medium, it's far less common for shows to be dubbed into other languages for international distribution.

For one thing, radio production is much less costly and complex than TV. So it's more likely that a foreign station will simply create a new show from scratch, rather than dub an existing U.S. show into their local tongue. And in most cases, foreign radio stations that carry U.S. shows are looking for the real thing. Their listeners want authenticity—including the original language presentation.

English is still considered a universal language. There are many millions of people overseas who understand English at least well enough to enjoy an American radio show. In some countries, such as the Philippines, English is the dominant language on both TV and AM radio. There are also ex-pats, U.S. workers, U.S. military, and American retirees in significant numbers in some foreign lands, who are eager to hear American radio shows. While Web radio has helped considerably in this regard, over-the-air radio broadcasts are still favored by many overseas listeners.

Lay of the Land

One thing that can stymie an international syndicator is the tangle of foreign media outlet variations that exist.

In some countries, for example, broadcast outlets are under state or national control. That doesn't necessarily mean they won't air your syndicated product. It just adds to the complexity of doing a deal, especially if you have to extract your payments from a government bureaucracy. Other countries have a mix of private and state-owned media. Still others have fully privatized media.

You may find yourself often haggling over terms with overseas folks. Some outlets will prefer to pay you weekly, others monthly, and still others annually. Others will suddenly vanish from the radar, after sticking with your show for many months. Did they decide to simply re-run all your previous content, without telling you? Unless you have a way to check up on them from thousands of miles away, you may never know.

Communicating with some foreign media contacts, even by email, can involve delays due to time zone and language considerations. But despite the obstacles, there is the potential for gaining overseas audiences and revenue from your content through international syndication.

Chapter 17 – Profiting from Your Content

You've created content and you've placed it on multiple outlets. In other words, you are now syndicated. So how and when do you start cashing in? This is where first-time syndicators sometimes fall short. This chapter explains some ways to monetize your efforts.

Network, Syndicate, or Agency

If you're syndicating under the auspices of a full service network or independent syndication firm, it's likely they already have a structure in place to generate revenue from your content. If you signed with a traditional network or print syndicate, you may already be earning a regular income or fee percentage from them. Most networks and syndicates have their own sales force, to generate revenue from ad sales or fee payments. If this is the case, income generation may not be an issue for you.

But if you are self-syndicating, or if you are just starting to establish an audience, you need to understand the syndication income sources.

Barter Syndication

Commercial radio and TV syndication in the U.S. employ a barter spot business model.

Barter was discussed in Chapter 4, but let's again explain what the term means. A certain number of ad positions within the syndicated content are reserved for each station to sell to their local advertisers, while the remaining ad slots are kept by the syndicator to sell to national advertisers.

In other words, the local outlet that accepts your show has bartered (traded) some of their advertising minutes to you, the syndicator, in exchange for the right to broadcast your show to their audience.

ROS Inventory and Cash

Depending on the structure of the deal between you and the station, the barter spots may air not just within the show itself. They may also run in other time periods on the station.

Ads that run in other "dayparts" (parts of the day) on a station are referred to as ROS (run of schedule) spots. Thus, a barter product might be offered to stations in exchange for in-show ad inventory, ROS inventory, or a combination of both.

Obviously, the more ad inventory you demand of the station, the greater your potential income. But stations are usually reluctant to add a show that requires a high number of barter spots.

If you're fairly new to syndication and you're going it alone, I suggest you try to learn what other shows with a similar structure are charging, and try to follow their lead. In any case, you'll soon find out if you're asking too much, because most station executives won't hesitate to tell you if they think you're overcharging.

Of course, if you work with a syndication consultant or industry mentor, they should be able to advise you on this important decision.

In some cases in radio and TV syndication, the station may also pay cash for a show. Alternatively, cash may be combined with barter spots. But cash is far less commonly paid unless a syndicated product is in high demand, or stations are competing within a market for the right to carry it.

In contrast to broadcast media, newspaper syndication is typically a fee-based cash deal. If you work with a syndicate, they will collect the fees from the papers and retain a share of this income, and you get the rest. If you self-syndicate, then you collect and keep 100% of the fees.

It's All in the Numbers

In most cases, a radio or TV syndicator ends up with a set number of barter ad minutes on each station on its network. For example, let's say your weekly show contains 5 minutes of barter inventory and your show is syndicated on 50 (or however many) stations. What you have is 5 minutes of network ad inventory. It's called "network inventory" simply because your station list comprises a radio network.

To most people, owning network ad inventory sounds impressive. And the reality is that it can be very impressive! The network radio and TV business is massive, and you have just become part of this industry.

So what are your network ad minutes worth? The answer to that question varies considerably. Your network barter ads might be worth a significant amount (for example, an annual income of six or seven figures). They might be worth considerably less than that—even virtually zero. It all depends on what sponsors will pay you for them!

The amount advertisers are willing to pay for your spots is based primarily upon the total size of your audience. However, your ability to sell the ads effectively is also a factor in their value. If you don't know how to sell commercials, and you can't get a third party to sell them for you, it will obviously be difficult to earn much from the spots.

Fortunately, there are individual salespeople, independent syndication firms, ad agencies, and other entities willing to sell your spots for you. And there are advertisers ready to pay sizable sums for national barter ads, once a syndicated show reaches a reasonable audience size.

Radio's total annual ad revenue is about $15 billion, while TV's yearly ad revenue is about $20 billion. These figures represent a combined total of local and national advertising sales figures.

Barter ads in syndicated shows are a part of this total broadcast revenue pie, and that share is in the multibillions of dollars. This sector has seen positive recent growth.

Major advertisers consistently invest large sums to buy spots in national shows, because that is an efficient way for them to reach many millions of people with their messages. Placing one spot in a nationally syndicated show will cost an advertiser significantly less than placing a local buy for that same spot in each individual market in which the show airs.

Reaching CM3

CM3 is our acronym for Critical Mass to Make Money. "Critical mass" refers to your audience share.

The key to tapping into the lucrative national advertising market is to grow your audience until it exceeds the critical-mass level. At that point it becomes measurable in terms of national rating share. This is the threshold at which your barter spots begin to have real marketable value. Once you reach this level, the basic value of your spots will double each time your audience doubles (moving from a 0.1 to 0.2 share, for example).

Recently launched syndicated shows usually haven't yet reached CM3. It takes more than just a few outlets to deliver a meaningful national audience.

This all-too-common scenario may be a challenge for the beginning syndicator, who may need cash income to pay for the marketing and distribution efforts. Unfortunately, there's usually not much income—particularly from ad sales—until the audience of the show reaches a reasonable size.

Alternative Sources of Income

What can you do in the meantime, while waiting for the product to hit CM3? There are a number of ways to convert unsold ad inventory into cash income during the early days, when your product is just getting established.

One of these tactics relies as much as anything on having a relationship with a potential advertiser or investor. In the case of an advertiser, your goal with an under-rated show is to convince them to jump in early as a charter advertiser.

It's to your benefit to make whatever deal is necessary to get the first sponsor aboard. Once that first advertiser has broken the ice, you'll find it's much easier to convince a second and third advertiser to try running some ads in your show.

There may be an opportunity to align yourself with an advertiser that fits the niche category of your syndicated content.

Let's say you do a syndicated show about pets. Perhaps there's a pet food company that would love to sponsor your show. We call such sponsors Affinity Advertisers, and they can become your longtime loyal supporters.

Product Endorsements and More

Assuming you've positioned yourself as a credible source, a sponsor might be willing to ante up in exchange for your endorsement of their product or service. Of course, you'll want to make sure their product measures up before you put your name behind it.

In some cases, advertisers might be willing to compensate you handsomely for editorial mentions, positive reviews, or even on-air interviews. Only you can best define the limits of how far to stretch your involvement with an advertiser, and how much to blur the line between content and paid messages. But we suggest caution here. The added income might not be worth risking your credibility with the audience and your media outlets.

Unsold Ad Inventory

Hosting a show with lots of unsold advertising time is like piloting a commercial plane with lots of empty seats. Once the show ends, that potential income is gone forever. So it makes sense to try to fill some of those "empty seats," even if it's for pennies on the dollar.

There are various firms that sell what are termed "remainder" ads and "per-inquiry" (PI) ads.

Remainder ads are usually priced very low. To use the above example, they're the equivalent of standby seating on an airplane. Remainder ads are most often used to fill unsold spot positions in rated shows, but they may also be available to run in a low-rated show.

Per-inquiry ads pay the syndicator based upon how many inquiries (phone calls or Web clicks) the ad generates for the advertiser. To track inquiries, each ad contains a unique response mechanism. For example, the spots in your show will include a specific phone number or Web address, so the exact results of your campaign can be tallied.

As with remainder ads, the revenue numbers with PI spots are somewhat unimpressive. However, these ads usually add a professional sound to your show, and they do generate some income—which is far better than earning nothing.

With either of these approaches, you should check out the ad firm beforehand. As in every industry, some companies are more reputable than others. Keep in mind that with any per-inquiry campaign, you rely on the firm's integrity to honestly report your income. This is because you have no way to know directly how many inquiries were generated by the ads that ran in your show.

Here's the bottom line. In most cases, the revenue from your content won't become meaningful until your audience reaches the minimum size for real national ad sales. So in the absence of a charter advertiser, investor, or some initial funds in the bank, the challenge for most start-up syndicators is to plan their budget carefully and persist in growing their show until it has a meaningful audience. Then they can start to see real income.

National Sales

A good way to quickly tap national revenue once you hit CM3 is to find a professional salesperson or organization to sell your advertising inventory. The seller might be an independent syndication firm, an ad sales network, or a regional or national advertising agency. Alternatively, you might work with a "one-man band" who is in the business of selling ads for a number of shows. The challenge in the latter case is to find someone who will consistently give your show the sales effort it deserves.

Most of the ad selling firms mentioned above will work with you on a commission basis—meaning they will retain a percentage of the sales income and you get the rest.

Once you set up such a relationship, your primary responsibility will be to ensure the ads they provide are inserted into your show properly and run as scheduled. Assuming the seller does their job, regular payment checks will arrive in your mailbox or be deposited directly into your bank account. When this starts to happen, it's a beautiful thing to behold.

Selling Your Content and Image

Once you create a syndication product in one medium, there's no reason you can't transfer it to other media. If your content is in written form, you might want to create a sponsored blog, an e-book (or traditional book), or a CD-ROM compilation. If your content is audio or video, you can market that as a hard product, too.

Do you realize you're a national expert in your field? Thanks to syndication, your name now carries weight. Why not hang up a shingle and become a consultant or advisor in your area of expertise?

You can also build a network of members who are willing to pay something to receive regular, personal updates from you—perhaps in the form of a club newsletter or some other information product you send them.

How did you waste time before the Internet?

Another idea is to create a membership website, with paid access. Typically, a certain percentage of your audience will be ready to take a chance and sign up for something new. Once they join your site, ask them for testimonials to encourage others to sign up, too.

Build a List

Top marketing experts suggest that anyone wanting to earn income long-term should start to build an email or snail mail list. You are in the perfect position to do this as a syndicator, because you have an audience interested in your content.

To get started building a list, you might offer a free gift or a free info product to your audience, in exchange for their email address. You will want to reassure them that you will not be sending them spam, or selling their email addresses to third parties, or otherwise abusing their privacy.

Once you get started with this project, you'll want to periodically stay in touch with the list members to avoid having the contacts grow stale. As the mailing list grows, you can periodically send out occasional product offers (perhaps for items you create), sponsor coupons, and other income generating items, along with frequent chunks of meaningful information and content.

Some money making Internet opportunities include CPC (cost per click) and CPA (cost per action) offers. With these deals, you receive a payment when a consumer clicks, signs up, or takes some action. Over time, a large list can generate significant revenue for you, assuming you manage it properly.

Multimillion dollar marketing empires have been built through little more than the skillful use of a large and well-cultivated email list. The possibilities here are beyond the scope of this book, but the idea might be worth exploring as a long-term income source.

Someone to Bankroll You

Funding to sustain you and get your syndicated product over the necessary starting hump can come from another source. You might solicit one or more investors to bankroll your entire syndication venture, before having to lay out the first dime on your own. Assuming you're passionate about your niche topic, you may be able to attract a like-minded potential investor to foot the bills for your effort.

An affluent person who strongly relates to your content could be a prime financial supporter. If you plan to go in this direction, be sure to have financial specifics worked out in advance. A reasonable investor will want to know that your dollar figures make sense, and that you're not grabbing numbers out of thin air.

To attract a worthy investor, consider preparing a written business plan. The business plan will show that you're serious about your syndication project, and that you've done the homework to show it is a viable concept.

Through the years, I've had many requests from syndicators for help in this area. That inspired me to create a full-length sample business plan for a syndicated radio show. It is customizable by revising the text sections and plugging in your numbers and a budget for the project. It can easily be adapted to media other than radio, including TV and the Internet.

This sample Syndication Business Plan is included in an advanced professional training course we created, titled *The Radio Syndication Academy*. You can find it at our online store at www.Syndication.net.

Soliciting Donations

Another way to raise funds is to ask your audience directly for financial support. This is a common approach for public radio and TV stations, which sustain themselves this way. Their station budgets are typically in the millions of dollars or higher, so the approach must work! If your audience seems to truly enjoy your content, why not ask them to lend support in the form of monetary contributions? Your syndication project is likely not a legally registered, nonprofit entity (meaning, donations are not tax-deductible), but your most loyal fans will probably be willing to throw a few dollars in the pot if you ask them.

Chapter 18 – The Nine Biggest Mistakes of Syndication

This chapter contains some of the most popular content we've ever offered on the topic of syndication. So we can hardly present a book on the subject of syndication without including it.

These nine lessons were originally written with radio syndication in mind, but we believe that they all apply to every form of media syndication in one way or another. For example, Mistake Number One refers to radio show demos. If radio isn't your thing, simply substitute the word "sample" for "demo" to see how the lesson applies to your particular type of content.

Mistake Number One: Submitting the Typical Demo

If you've ever visited one of those gourmet grocery stores, you've probably nibbled some free samples of goodies at the little tables they set up in the aisles.

It's a fact—sampling is a great way to sell products in the food biz. Once people get a taste, they often feel compelled to buy the product on the spot.

On the other hand, putting up posters or handing out fliers has far less impact on shoppers. If you go directly to the pleasure center of their brain, by giving a yummy taste of the product, that works wonders.

What's this got to do with your syndicated show?

Well, here's the point. You can build the most impressive web site, design the coolest logo, dream up the cleverest name and concept for your show. But what really cuts through and convinces a radio station to add your show is just one thing: the demo.

In radio syndication, hearing is believing. It's sort of like giving away a tasty food sample. It's your one big chance to get right inside their brain and make a real impression.

And it's also where most show demos fail miserably.

Anyone who's been program director of a radio station knows that the vast majority of show demos they receive are lame at best, and often painfully bad. These are what we call the "typical" show demos.

Typical demos cause station executives to switch off, mentally. Not to mention switch off your demo. In a few brief moments, they make a decision regarding your show. If you have a typical demo, chances are their decision isn't a happy one.

Now, don't let this news intimidate you. Actually, the fact that most demos are so typically bad should make you feel good. Once you understand how to create a NON-typical demo, you will be way ahead of the competition.

First, what is a typical demo? Physically, it's an audio file, or perhaps a compact disc. That much is perfectly fine.

The typical mp3 demo usually has a typical file name: demo.mp3, show_demo, my_demo, etc. This makes perfect sense to the demo creator, since it's their demo!

But just about every station executive we know of has a dozen or more unidentifiable mp3 files sitting on their hard drive with names like "demo" or something equally typical.

And you don't want to be typical, right?

How about compact disc demos? Well, the typical CD demo has a title scrawled on it with a sharpie. Or even worse, the surface is completely blank. So, NOT being typical means properly labeling your CD demo disc. At the very least, put your name and phone number on the CD. How long does this take? Less than 30 seconds. Yet in our experience, very few seem to bother with it.

Moving right along...what about sound quality?

Typical demos contain distractions such as hiss, hum, clicks, buzzing, or static. They may sound muffled or garbled. Don't expect a station executive to "listen past" the lousy quality, even if you warn them about it in advance. That's like interviewing for an important job with a nasty stain on your shirt, and telling the interviewer to please ignore the stain. Too late—a sloppy impression has been made.

We've heard show hosts say, "But this is my very best show! It may have lousy technical quality, but this is my best one!"

Go back to the example of the job interview. Imagine telling the recruiter, "Sorry about this ugly stain, but this is my very best shirt. So I had to wear it!" Does this give you a sense of how a demo with lousy sound quality might come across to station decision-makers?

Now let's get to what matters most: the actual content of your show demo. This is the part that really counts, and it's where typical demos always fall short.

Over the years, we've read scientific estimates of the average human being's attention span. We've also seen studies of how long it takes to make an impression with someone you meet for the first time. The fact is, it takes only seconds before a person decides what they think of you. And once that impression is made, it's hard to change it.

A similar process happens when a station executive begins to listen to your show demo. We've seen program directors make a snap decision about a demo in a few seconds. However, most PDs are more professional than that, and will give it a decent listen before making a decision.

To most station execs, your syndicated show demo offers the enticing promise of more listeners, higher ratings, and more sales. They're really hoping your show will knock their socks off, and that your demo WON'T be typical.

A great demo is a combination of art and science. It has to grab the jaded listener with something compelling, something entertaining, perhaps something clever and funny—and all within the first few moments.

Then, it needs to do that again. And again, before it ends. It should make at least three great impressions on the listener, and maybe more. That's the effective formula we've seen work time and again to convince a station executive to add a show.

It's just like a busy grocery shopper, who has a taste of something yummy still lingering in their brain. They instinctively grab the product right off the shelf. You must get stations to add YOUR show in the same instinctive way!

We've heard thousands of "typical" syndicated show demos over the last few decades, and not very many great ones.

The Bottom Line: Don't be typical. Create your very own great demo—one that makes station executives sit up, smile, and sign up!

Mistake Number Two: Contacting Big Stations—the Wrong Way

We suppose Mistake Number Two is caused by human nature.

Most show hosts who launch a radio show into syndication have high expectations. Their fondest desire is to see their show dazzle the nation and make a huge media impact. Their goal is to get on the air in big cities like New York, Los Angeles, Chicago, Philadelphia, Boston, San Francisco, Dallas, DC, Atlanta, and Houston as soon as possible.

Obviously, a station in New York or Chicago can deliver far more audience and potential revenue for a syndicator than a station in East Elbow, Arkansas. It might take 1,000 tiny stations or more to equal the reach of just one major market affiliate.

So it's no surprise to see an eager first-time syndicator get on the phone and start dialing and smiling, hoping to sign a big market right out of the box.

This approach is a big mistake, for several reasons.

First, it's a serious waste of time. If your show is new and nationally unproven, no major market station executive in their right mind will ever consider adding it right away.

A gatekeeper will likely give you the bad news that their boss isn't interested, and you may even hear the classic line, "Don't call us, we'll call you," followed by the phone slamming down.

It's not that they're rude—big stations are often overloaded with syndicators, PR flacks, promoters, and others all trying to pitch new, mostly unproven shows, products, guests, books, etc.

Think about it. How did these station executives successfully climb the ladder to run top stations? They did it by being smart, by avoiding risk, by managing time, and by making good decisions. The higher they rose in the industry, the more careful they got about every decision.

Don't let this discourage you! Major market stations add syndicated shows all the time. But recognize that the decision-maker will want to see proof of performance—a track record of station signings. This dramatically lowers the risk of adding your show to their station.

So how do you quickly get that track record?

The answer is simple. The road to major markets runs through medium and small markets. Stations in lesser markets have far lower resistance to new ideas.

We believe some of the most exciting and entertaining radio is heard in America's medium and small markets, simply because these stations enjoy taking a chance on shows that aren't yet proven. In addition, these decision-makers are often easier to get on the phone than their big-city counterparts. They're also more willing to listen to your pitch, and more likely to add your new show.

The most logical syndication strategy is to first build your station list in medium and small markets. If you sign up a few markets per week, in a year you will have 100 or more stations in your network. That's very impressive, and it will make even the biggest major markets take notice.

What really grabs the attention of major markets is MOMENTUM. Let executives know that your show has a steady track record of station growth, and they may begin taking your calls—and, even more importantly, adding your syndicated show.

Mistake Number Three: Asking Them for Too Much

This one's fairly subtle, but it's important. Let me paint a picture to explain.

You've been asking a certain top station to add your show. Finally, you're almost there! The station decision-maker is seriously considering your show for their next opening. Or maybe the decision-maker has already shared exciting news with you: They need a show just like yours, and you have a "99% done deal" with them!

Good for you! No doubt you're picturing that signed agreement arriving in your email or on the fax. You're thinking of the press release you'll put out to announce the news. You're smiling as you think about celebrating this big addition, perhaps with a special night out with family or friends.

Then out of the blue, the station executive calls you back.

With a sheepish-sounding voice, they quickly tell you they're really sorry, but the station has decided to go in another direction. Maybe they'll reconsider your show later. "Please stay in touch, yada yada, thanks and again, we're sorry, goodbye."

If you're quick, you might get in a question or two before the call ends. "What changed your minds about adding my show? Everything looked so promising! What happened?"

The response may be vague. "You have a great show...it's nothing personal...there are some things we're dealing with here...I can't get into it right now...we're just not able to pull the trigger...my boss changed his mind unexpectedly...the owner doesn't want to do it...."

Whatever.

The call ends, but you still don't know exactly what happened. You've just been shot down, and you're feeling confused and frustrated.

Truth be told, there could be many causes for the rejection. But when a deal blows up at this point in the process, it's possible to guess the specific cause. Probably the station executive (or a boss, or the station owner) finally got around to reading your syndication agreement closely. Most busy station people usually don't do this until moments before they sign the deal.

If there was something in the terms that turned off the decision-maker or the boss or the station owner—or even their attorney, it often triggers an out-of-the-blue rejection like this one.

What's especially frustrating is that you no doubt would have bent the terms of the deal if only they'd asked. And some stations WILL actively negotiate with you, rather than back out. Some stations will even rewrite your agreement and then tell you to take it or leave it.

But most people find negotiating to be unpleasant and uncomfortable. Think about the last time you bought a car. Did you enjoy the negotiation process? If you did, you're one in a thousand.

There are many different ways to structure a syndication deal. Maybe another show the station uses has better terms than yours. So, while your deal may be perfectly fair in your eyes, the station decision-maker (or others behind the scenes), may have decided you wanted too much. Rather than haggle with you, it may be easier for them to just move on and find another show.

This scenario most often occurs when a show is just getting established—when stations don't see it as a "must-have." Once a show gets fully established, stations are more amenable to what the syndicator wants. But if your show is in the critical first year, it's important to be flexible and very fair with your agreement.

Let's look at a common sticking point in radio syndication agreements. In the world of business, one of the most common term lengths for a contract is one year. That's when both parties agree to stay with it for a minimum of 12 months. This is so commonplace that if you ask the average attorney to draw up a syndication contract for your show, we predict they'll suggest it have a minimum one-year term.

Now I'm not a lawyer, I don't pretend to be one on TV, and I don't dish out legal advice. If you need legal advice, see a real attorney. But in our experience, a one-year term is too long, if a show is still getting established. So you must be flexible with the term length. This will lower the station's risk level in adding your show. The result? More stations will sign up, with less resistance.

What's the best term length? The answer depends on the type of show you do. And it's just one of many things to consider in setting terms in your show's syndication agreement.

By the way, we've found that being flexible in your syndication agreement doesn't impact your long-term results. Once your show gets added by a station, the odds are good that it will stay on the station. The challenge is getting it on stations in the first place! That's why you need to be flexible from the start.

Mistake Number Four: Relying on the Web for All Your Marketing

Unless you've been living in a cave or on another planet, you've no doubt heard comments like these time and again, over the past decade or so:

- "Internet marketing has changed everything."
- "The Web has transformed our daily lives."
- "The online world has revolutionized business."
- "The Internet is the greatest thing since those little pre-packaged slices of cheese that cost too darn much but I'm too lazy to cut slices of it myself."

Okay, maybe you never heard that last comment, but we're sure the others sound familiar.

And all of these statements are true, to an extent. Many consider the Internet (and Internet marketing) to be incredible boons for business. There's an entire industry specializing in the intricacies, tricks, and techniques of Internet marketing. And of course, titans like Google, Yahoo, Amazon, and others built empires using the power of Internet marketing and sales.

We remember interviewing a certain business maven, back in the 1990s. He was a guest on one of our syndicated radio shows. This guy marveled at how Amazon.com carefully tracked the books he'd looked at on their site, and when he returned later (he was literally gasping with excitement at this point), they would offer him similar titles! And if he hadn't returned to their site in a while, they'd even send him emails about specific products he'd find interesting!

Most of us forget that this kind of marketing was once considered revolutionary. Today, this kind of Web and email marketing is fairly commonplace. Many online consumers have come to expect it.

With all the sophisticated tools of Web marketing now readily available, along with email, Facebook, Twitter, and YouTube, it seems obvious that the Internet should be the cornerstone of the growth strategy for your syndicated show. Right?

Wrong.

We think it's a bad idea to depend on only the Web and email to market your show to stations, for two big reasons.

First, almost everyone else in syndication is using the Internet and email to market their shows to radio stations—especially those shows with limited marketing budgets. Using the same marketing channels as everyone else is an ideal way to blend in, when what you need to do is stand out!

Second, all the key station decision-makers have learned effective ways to filter most Internet and email marketing communications. If you can't get their attention, nothing is going to happen for you.

For these reasons, we believe the most effective plan for marketing your show to radio stations should include not only Web marketing and email, but also every other communication channel at your disposal. And this doesn't mean spending a lot, either.

For example, regular, old-fashioned snail mail can still be remarkably effective. But your mail must stand out from the pile of mail that arrives each day at radio stations. Here are some simple ways to make this happen: Try an uncommonly bright color for the envelope. Use an oversize window envelope, which partially reveals something inside. Hand-scribble a provocative teaser message on the envelope.

Properly used, these simple but rarely used approaches will get your package noticed and opened, which is half the battle. Now your compelling marketing materials in the envelope can take over—and here's where you use the Internet to point the intrigued decision-maker to your online audio, video, and other materials.

Another incredibly powerful marketing tool? The old-fashioned telephone. But try to market a syndicated show by phone, and you'll run into voicemail or a gatekeeper (such as a harried assistant). Many syndicators deal with these roadblocks the same old way. They'll leave a predictable message, which (predictably) never gets returned.

Here's where smart syndicators employ what we like to call "proven telephone tricks and techniques" to make these roadblocks work for them, not against them. For example, just one key voicemail technique can boost callbacks by 50%.

We cover these tactics in more detail in our advanced professional information product, *The Radio Syndication Academy*. It's available at www.Syndication.net.

Most people only leave a name, number, and brief message. This is NOT the way to get your calls returned! Got a decision-maker on the phone? Use an arsenal of marketing tools, not just one. Permission-based marketing will keep you "top of mind" until they are ready to sign.

The phone helps forge a connection that can pay off nicely for you later. You usually can't build a personal connection like this through Internet marketing. But combining traditional marketing with the Web can be powerfully effective.

Mistake Number Five: Outsourcing—the Wrong Way

We've heard so many sad stories over the years about this one that it might be better to describe it as a Humongous Mistake, rather than just one of the Biggest Mistakes.

We're talking about the critical decision made by an idealistic show host or producer to blindly hand over some (or all) of the heavy lifting work of syndication to an outside party, and simply hope for the best.

Basically, the wrong choice here can result in frustration, financial pain, angry radio stations, unhappy listeners, missed opportunities, slow growth, lost prestige, damage to your brand image, utter shock and devastation, and possibly, complete nuclear annihilation.

OK, that last one may be a slight exaggeration. Your show may not end up getting totally destroyed in a giant fireball. But at the very least, you may feel like going to the nearest drinking establishment and getting bombed yourself, just to ease the pain.

When things go wrong and begin spinning out of control, it can be extremely upsetting. Clearly, it's far better NOT to make the mistake of choosing the wrong partner when you outsource some or all of your show's syndication efforts.

Now here's the good news. You're about to learn some ways to inoculate yourself against such a horrible mistake. But first, how can a disaster like this happen in the first place?

Radio and Internet media syndication is a multibillion dollar industry, and there are many large, well-established, trustworthy players in the business. There are also quite a few smaller, under-financed, and frankly less-than-professional service providers and resellers on the fringes. Please do not let this fact put you off from syndicating your radio show. Broadcast syndication, Internet media, and other forms of syndication are all truly fantastic businesses.

We've seen many, many show hosts succeed and thrive in these fields. It can be very rewarding and gratifying, giving you the lifestyle you've always dreamed of having for yourself and your family.

We suppose it's the same with any thriving industry. There are the winners—the healthy, successful, and well-respected companies, which have many satisfied customers. However, there are also the flakes—the ones you'd be better off avoiding. And it's not hard to avoid them, if you know what to watch out for.

As you'd expect, the less reputable players must compete aggressively for new business, in order to hang on and keep going. So, they're always trolling for new customers. And new radio hosts and newly syndicated shows are prime prospects. No surprise there—that's how the flakes manage to stay in business.

For example, they constantly scan lists of newly published books, because authors are prime targets for these scammers. They'll call you out of the blue to say your book is amazing, and now they want to offer you the chance to host a radio show! They do not bother to tell you upfront that you'll be paying for the privilege. You don't find that out until after you've gotten emotionally hooked on the idea of doing a show.

A few of these folks even own local radio stations, primarily for added credibility in recruiting new victims. They'll smother you with praise, flattery, and promises of fame: "You'll be heard on our high-powered station, along with our stellar lineup of major syndicated stars!" However, you'll also pay through the nose for airtime, you'll be told to "phone it in"—so audio quality will be marginal, and your time slot will be among the lowest rated of the week.

Taking this hype one step further, there's the promise of effortless wealth via the Internet. This big-juicy-pot-of-gold-at-the-end-of-the-rainbow mentality has attracted a variety of wannabe's and unknowns to the field of online radio and video.

You can probably see that novice show hosts and show producers face a potential minefield when it comes to choosing one or more reputable partners to help them syndicate and distribute their show.

You may be asking, "So why don't you just tell me the names of some companies to avoid?"

Sorry, no can do. Please understand that this would be like painting a big red target on the roof for every two-bit lawsuit jockey.

But we'll do the next best thing. We'll give you the perfect recipe for hiring the WRONG company, the kind that will drain your pocketbook and wreck your show (or at least slow you way down).

First, hire a company or an individual based on an unsolicited email or random phone call you happen to get. Especially if you hear loads of flattery about how great your voice is, or how wonderful your show will sound. (You're an author? They'll rave about your fabulous book, too.)

Let's face it. If a company has to actively cold-call new prospects in a field as competitive as syndication, how qualified can they be? If they have to search for customers, their services aren't in very high demand. And do you really want to work with them?

At the very least, they're experiencing lots of customer turnover, and need to replace the fleeing clients with new ones to stay afloat. In any case, consider it a red flag if a company approaches you.

As an aside, we suggest caution with ANY company that cold-calls you—pitching office supplies, insurance, listings in a business directory, etc. We suppose some are legit. But if they're decent, why do they need to make cold calls?

Next in our formula for failure: Always outsource your syndication to the company that charges you the least—especially if their price is WAY below all the others.

The fact is, quality marketing, production, distribution, and ad sales cost money. These services involve a real output of time and labor. So if someone promises to do it for pennies—or even nickels—that should shoot off a blazing magnesium warning flare.

That old saying applies to syndication: You get what you pay for.

Here's another way to hire the wrong company: Just go with your gut and sign up with the first person who says they love your show, or who has a really cool website, or just sounds really, really sincere. If these reasons to choose a vendor sound silly, we're sorry to say we've heard all of them directly from some sad hosts who made bad choices.

Another recipe for disaster, especially when outsourcing your syndication marketing, is neglecting to ask who does the outbound telemarketing. You just assume they're well-trained, in-house employees. The reality is sometimes far less impressive. A company may use unpaid college interns to call stations on your behalf. Or people scattered around the country (or overseas), working from their kitchen tables or a boiler room.

If you think this seems okay, imagine what a station executive thinks when someone calls to pitch your show, and in the background are the sounds of a yapping dog, a crying baby, a doorbell, or a beeping microwave.

Would that impact the image of your show? Do we even have to ask?

Understand, we have nothing against people who work from home. We've worked from home ourselves, in years past. But if you are paying a company for professional representation in the image-conscious media business, shouldn't the people marketing your show come across as totally professional? We've heard stories from station execs about scary calls they sometimes get from fringe syndicators. Needless to say, the impression isn't forgotten.

Moving right along, here are a few more hints about how to pick a bad vendor.

When hiring an outside firm to help you syndicate your show, be sure NOT to ask to see client testimonials. Don't ask them how long they've been in business, either. Don't ask if they have incoming toll-free numbers for stations to call. Don't ask if it's a one-man band or a "virtual" company.

If you're seeking to syndicate on Internet radio, don't visit their website to see if it's easy to navigate, if it has outdated or broken links, and if the audio of the shows sounds tinny or fuzzy.

If you're seeking ad sales, don't ask if they actually bring in cash revenue for their shows. Don't ask for names of actual sponsors.

Last but not least, if you sign with a radio syndicator, don't ask if they've placed any shows in major markets. That way, you'll be certain YOUR show will never be heard in a major market, either!

There you have it...the perfect recipe for a lot of pain and suffering! Hopefully you've learned that it isn't very hard to find a quality partner to help you find syndication nirvana. You just have to know the right questions to ask.

Mistake Number Six: Planning—What's That?

We remember seeing a funny poster years ago, on the wall of a classroom. In big bold red letters, it said: AVOID PROBLEMS...ALWAYS PLAN AHEAD!

But the words were too big. This forced the word "ahead" to be all scrunched over and bent along the right edge, just so it would fit on the poster.

The obvious joke: They're warning you to plan ahead, but they didn't follow their own advice.

The obvious message: Want to end up scrunched over and bent? Don't plan!

As the old saying goes, "Plan your work, and work your plan." This is always a smart idea when you're syndicating your radio show.

Okay, we can sense some eyes glazing over. For many of us creative types, planning sounds dull. It seems about as much fun as getting a root canal.

We're sure some folks are thinking, isn't radio about being spontaneous? What happened to FUN? Why not stay open and free to whatever the wonderful universe brings us?

We have no problem with any of that. Go ahead and be wild, crazy, and totally unpredictable when it comes to hosting your radio show. But if you want to avoid frustration as you grow the business side of your show, then some planning is essential.

Hosting a syndicated broadcast radio show or an Internet radio show can be a real blast. But we're sure you wouldn't mind making a profit, too! How much you pocket may depend on how good your planning is.

When you boil it all down, syndicating a radio show isn't much different from running a business. First, the syndicator (that's you) has a product: the show itself. Second, you have customers (actually, two sets of customers): your listeners and your advertisers.

Just like a business, if your product is good enough to attract customers, you can earn an income. And if your product attracts enough customers, you can earn a huge income!

But let's forget about your show and syndication for a moment. Instead, simply think any kind of business. Think of a car dealership, a big box retailer, a hair salon, a restaurant, whatever.

Imagine how any of these businesses might plan things to maximize their results and succeed in a big way.

If they're smart, the owner will carefully search for the best location, and make sure it's ideal for attracting the right kinds of customers. They'll try to design their store to be as customer-friendly as possible, and they'll create signage and an engaging color scheme that gets noticed—one that communicates the right message to the folks they want to attract. If they're not experts at this stuff, they might ask a few professionals to handle these tasks for them.

Hopefully, the new store owner will also check out the competition, just to see how others in the niche are doing. That info will help the business owner figure out how their store will best fit into the existing marketplace, and how they can beat the competition at serving people.

Business owners should also take the time to ask themselves a few hard questions. What special and unique attributes does my new store bring to the market? What sets me apart from the rest? How can I fine-tune and sharpen my product to make it even more attractive to customers?

Promotion and marketing are also worth planning. The business owner might engage a marketing company to assist them, if they're not sure how to do it. Again, it may help to see what other successful owners are doing, and pattern a strategy after their winning behavior.

Now, if the store owner has done their homework and planned well, chances are their new store will be a big hit on opening day, and keep growing and making a profit for many years to come.

But if they haven't done much planning—if they just go into it hoping things will work out—then they're taking a gamble. The store owner might get lucky and find many customers, but it's likely that things will be less successful than if they'd taken the time to plan a little bit.

Let's now consider YOUR syndicated radio show.

Do you think some planning might help to ensure your success, given the factors we've just discussed? Are you at risk of getting scrunched over and bent, like the words on that poster, by not planning ahead? (Ouch—hate when that happens!)

The bottom line: A little planning goes a long way.

It may seem like overkill, but the extra effort of creating a written business plan for your syndicated radio show is a smart idea. A business plan will walk you through the process of answering all the key questions on paper. It will also help you explore all the expense and profit factors in syndication before they occur.

Perhaps you've wondered how quickly you'll break even, how much you'll earn, or what your costs will be. These things can all be projected with some accuracy, with a well-written business plan.

And if you hope to find an investor to fund the launch of your show, you'll definitely need a written business plan. Investors love to see a business plan because it tells them you're serious about what you're doing.

If you're self-syndicating your show, or if profits aren't critical to you, having a written plan may not be necessary. But it's still worth taking the time to work through your options on paper. Think about your goals in national radio syndication and Internet syndication. A bit of foresight could help you avoid missteps.

Before we wrap up this lesson, here are some pithy phrases for your planning portfolio (try saying that three times, fast):

- Plan ahead! Remember, it wasn't raining when Noah built the ark.
- Well begun...is half done.

- If you don't have a plan, you'll end up being part of someone else's.

Mistake Number Seven: Calling Your Show NEW

What's that old saying? We think it goes, "Everything old is new again."

We suppose there's truth in that saying. Especially thanks to Botox, Viagra, and breast implants.

But if you want to be a sure winner in broadcast radio and Internet syndication, skip the pills and surgery and try a different saying: "Everything new isn't new...and it isn't old, either. It just IS!"

Calling a show NEW is one little syndication screw-up we uncovered years ago. Prominent use of this word is an even greater marketing mistake today than it used to be, due to industry consolidation. We'll explain in a moment.

We've kept this mistake to ourselves for a long time, happy to let others use the word NEW to degrade their marketing efforts. And they do use it, over and over again.

However, calling a show "new" is one of the least obvious and most common errors, even among the biggest and most experienced syndicators and networks. That's because calling any radio show "new" is a negative, even if it IS new to syndication.

Yet we suppose it's no surprise that many syndicators like to use this term to describe their syndicated shows, especially at the beginning of the syndication process. After all, most advertising experts embrace "new" as one of the power marketing words. We've read many books about product marketing. All said it's a mistake NOT to use the word "new" in many cases, even if a product has been around for years. They tell you to reinvent your product more often than pop star Lady Gaga changes her wardrobe, and to market your product with blurbs like "new formula" or "new flavor."

246

We invite you to take a leisurely stroll through the aisles of a nearby grocery store, pharmacy, big-box retail franchise, discount warehouse club, or any of the other temples of mass consumerism that are liberally scattered across the landscape.

You'll see item upon item and label after label featuring a word balloon, sunburst, or day-glo sticker screaming NEW in bold, italicized, underlined, or drop-shadowed fonts. Consumers are well-programmed to grab anything on the shelf that shouts NEW at them.

"New" is a motivating word when it comes to selling stuff to consumers. It's also a power word people use every day to provoke the interest of their fellow human beings.

- "Hey, I got an NEW job!"
- "There's a NEW movie opening Friday...wanna see it?"
- "They opened a NEW steak joint...let's go!"
- "We just had a NEW baby!"
- "Do you like my NEW hair style?"

And so on.

So if it's such a great word, why do we say NEW is a no-no in syndication?

Here's why. Program directors and station executives are happiest when they have ratings and revenue. Internet radio networks are happiest when they have traffic and revenue.

What drives ratings, traffic, and revenue? Quality shows and hosts. Unproven programs and hosts do not have the same positive effect, simply because they are new and unproven. This may seem obvious. But stay with me here.

Consider people in the media industry, specifically those who make programming decisions. They're the ones who will decide whether YOUR show will be added to their stations or networks.

Your show will either grow or shrink, depending on what these people decide.

These decision-makers are in the game to win. They have survived and fought their way to key positions, in part because they've learned to be very smart about risk. Their daily choices determine their future. If they make bad choices, ratings and revenue will plunge, and they will get booted out the door.

In life, there can be a thrill in risk taking. That's why most of us enjoy a little risk from time to time. It may be trying a new soft drink, riding a scary roller coaster, or skydiving. It all depends on what we consider risky fun.

But media decision-makers carefully weigh the potential cost of every risk. Media survivors (those who've made it to a level where they can add new shows) are very savvy about risk taking.

Compare this to the risk of a consumer who buys a box of cereal that says NEW on the label. What's his or her risk—that the cereal won't be crunchy? The consumer gets a small kick from trying something new for breakfast, but a bad cereal decision won't destroy their career.

But in an industry where people are fired when ratings slip by one tenth of a ratings point, a NEW show gives something more like a quiver of fear. It's best to go with something NOT NEW, something with signs of acceptance, something that's proven. So the word NEW can actually be a red flag to station executives to NOT add your show.

Then what's the answer, if you have a NEW syndicated show? Based on our experience, we believe it's always best to market your show—even if it IS brand–new—as a proven winner, one that the industry already embraces.

How do you do this? There are a number of ways. Here are a few of them:

248

- Convince a few friendly station executives to provide endorsements for your show. Use these blurbs prominently in your marketing. These quotes are seen by others as signs that your show has industry acceptance, even though it may not be heard on many stations yet.

- Market your show through a known syndicator or network. This lends an immediate mantle of recognition and authority. If you work with a decent firm, many stations already have a working relationship with them and your show will naturally become part of that association.

- Use proven marketing angles. When presenting your show to stations, use proper industry lingo. The right buzzwords not only signal that you know what you're doing, but can also lend your show a certain aura of authority, when it comes time to consider adding it. Avoid words that turn them off (yes, one of them is NEW). And don't let your marketing be too outside the norm, or it may put them off your show completely.

We recently did some math. Of the shows we've syndicated, 74% were brand-new (or almost brand-new) when they came to us. We never used the word "new" to describe any of them! Whether your show is new or not, you can put it in the winner's circle by always keeping the station decision-maker's point of view in mind.

Mistake Number Eight: Giving Up Too Soon

If you're planning to syndicate a radio show, or you're already in syndication but you're not earning a profit yet, just how much time should you realistically give yourself? What's a reasonable time line, in terms of giving your syndicated show a real shot at success?

Take a guess at what we most often hear from beginners in radio syndication. What do you think they say is a good time frame to decide whether to keep forging ahead, or throw in the towel?

If you guessed "six months," bingo. That's what many beginners believe is the right amount of time to know whether their show is going to survive and thrive in syndication.

Okay—we suppose everyone wants fast results these days. But six months for syndication success? You can't find a car dealer who'll lease you a set of wheels for less than 30 months. And yet people think they can measure the success or failure of a syndicated radio show in six months?

Well, guess what—a year may not be enough time, either.

Major syndicators take a very different view of things. And no doubt that's how they got to be such big syndicators in the first place. When starting a new syndicated show, the major syndicators often create a five-year business plan. Five years!

And of course, they also make adjustments and evaluations every step of the way, just as any smart syndicator should do. Yes, even the big guns expect a few trials and tribulations in the early stages of a show's national growth. This is to be expected in any competitive field, including syndication.

When a nationally syndicated radio show proves successful, the rewards can be enormous. And there are many independent shows that earn their hosts plenty of money. These are the hosts who stayed with it through their early uncertainties.

Our first syndicated show, *The Success Journal*, went national almost 20 years ago, and it's still going strong today. It grew from being broadcast on just one lonely station at 4 a.m. Sunday mornings, to running on 150 broadcast stations and American Forces radio worldwide, and it airs five days a week.

Did *The Success Journal* achieve all this in year one? Absolutely not. It wasn't until year two that it really began to pull in a substantial profit. And here's the beauty part of syndication. This show has continued to generate revenue since our early commitment to it, year after year after year. Once we got it on enough stations, the show began to generate a significant income that continues to this day.

Somewhere, we still have that 36-month wall chart created to track the initial station signings. It wasn't a straight line, either. There were quite a few plateaus between the times when stations were signing up.

Years later, we launched a second syndicated show, *InfoTrak*, which is now closing in on 600 stations. This weekly show also earns a steady income. Just like *The Success Journal*, there is steady income from *InfoTrak* every month. By the way, the bumpy economy hasn't affected the income from these shows much, because large-volume advertisers see genuine value in national radio. It's a very efficient way to reach a mass audience, so the ads continue to sell in good economic times as well as bad.

Just as with the first show, we had to invest in *InfoTrak* for a period of time before it started producing income. The show didn't hit its stride until after year one.

So it's not just the giant "alphabet" networks that are making money in this business. Smart, persistent show hosts can earn substantial incomes while having fun and enjoying the recognition that comes from being a syndicated show host. A successful show can provide you with the ideal lifestyle you've always wanted. You can live anywhere you wish, while enjoying loads of free time for family and all the things that matter to you.

But here's the mandatory disclaimer: Syndication is NOT a get–rich-quick scheme. You could earn a lot, a little, or nothing. You could even lose money. Many factors determine success or failure. Isn't that the way it is with everything in life?

Some time ago, talk host Rush Limbaugh signed a long term deal with his syndicator, valued in the hundreds of millions. What the news stories didn't mention is that his *first* year in syndication wasn't so rosy. Rush struggled to get affiliates in major markets in year one. This was clear to me as the manager of a radio station back in 1988. Our station was one of his early adopters (because we guessed that his show, being so unique, would grab a sizable audience -- and it did).

Back then, Rush's syndicator begged us to pick it up. They were thrilled when we finally agreed to carry the talk show.

Now what if Rush had measured his progress based upon year one, where would he be today? Probably nowhere!

As explained in our *Joy of Syndication* Audio Seminar, imagine a farmer who has just planted 40 acres. To a non-farmer, it looks like nothing is happening. The vast field looks like a big, empty bunch of dirt. It looks pretty bleak if you don't understand farming.

But unseen to everyone, the seeds that the farmer planted will soon sprout. And, eventually, that farmer will enjoy a bountiful harvest if he stays with it and patiently tends his field.

On the other hand, if the farmer quits too soon, he'll harvest nothing. He won't even recoup the time and cost of planting all those seeds in the first place.

In syndication, the "seeds" are the demos you've sent to stations, the calls you've made to Program Directors, the emails you've blasted out, the word of mouth and the buzz, the press releases, and so on. You must allow time for all those seeds to sprout.

There are instances where a station finally decides to add a syndicated show, only to discover that the show is no longer in syndication because the host decided things weren't happening fast enough.

Perhaps a program director is awaiting approval to add new shows. Maybe a station is changing format, or is tied up with a research project. It may be their annual budget process, or whatever. It can take time for stations to make a decision.

So, as you make your plans, think big. Give your show a chance for real growth. And give yourself the best information and support system possible, to ensure you take the right steps.

Mistake Number Nine: Waiting Until Everything Is Perfect

Here we go with Mistake Number 9, and this one's a doozy. Why? Because it's a wrong way of thinking that messes with people's dreams and goals.

If you've gotten all the way to Mistake Number 9, we're guessing that you're someone who is serious about the idea of syndicating your show.

You know what? You're not alone. Not by a long shot.

The endless, ongoing fascination with syndication does not surprise me one bit. Over the years, we've communicated with countless numbers of people who had the very same dreams about syndication that you have.

Radio syndication truly gives you a platform to share your thoughts, hopes, and dreams with millions of people. And of course, a syndicated show can also make you money.

A few of the top syndicated hosts have eight-figure contracts. Frankly, it's unlikely you'll earn quite that much, but many syndicated hosts with decent-sized national audiences do earn five, six, or seven figure incomes.

And you can host a live show from just about anywhere. Thanks to all the cool technology today, all the broadcast gear you need fits in a carry-on bag. We know of syndicated hosts who broadcast their shows from beach homes, luxury hotels, and even tropical islands and cruise ships. Some hosts enjoy free travel, hotel, and other perks for themselves and their families, just by doing shows on-location at resorts and other destinations.

And how about simply hosting the show from the comfort of your home? Long daily commutes instantly become a thing of the past. You can even do the show in your pajamas if you want, since nobody can see you on radio.

So with all those benefits to recommend syndication, why aren't more people pursuing their dream?

Among the many people we've advised, one common roadblock stops many of them. It's the idea that their show has to be perfect before it can be launched nationally. We're here to tell you: Nothing could be further from the truth!

Your show does NOT have to be perfect. Nor do the circumstances have to be perfect, either. If you think the present economy is a bad time to start a nationally syndicated show, you're wrong. Bad economic times are precisely when stations are open to syndication, because it's a way for them to save money.

Besides, if you think things have to be perfect, guess what? Things will NEVER be perfect, and you'll never take the first step.

Our first show, *The Success Journal*, was not that great to begin with. In fact, the earliest shows are truly cringeworthy. But we believe some real passion for the topic came through, and that's what convinced stations to sign up and carry it.

It was the same with the second show we launched years later, *InfoTrak*. The early shows were far from perfect. By the time of the *InfoTrak* launch, however, we'd learned not to worry so much. Both shows now sound better than they used to, but neither of them is flawless. Consider them works in progress.

So here's a good formula for success in syndication:

75% (Implementation and Action, with Passion) + 25% (Creation and Ongoing "Perfecting" of Your Show) = 100% (Success in Syndication)

In other words, most of your success comes from TAKING ACTION!

You must set aside any fears of failure, and stop worrying that your show isn't good enough for a national audience. You must stop "waiting for the right time to come along" to make the leap into syndication, and just jump in and go for it.

The reason the current crop of broadcasters have made it on the air is very simple: They chased their dreams. YOU can do just as well (or better) than them, but it will never happen unless you take action. There are only two keys: Create a show about whatever ignites your passion and interest, and then FOLLOW THROUGH with the right action steps.

Not every syndicated show will be a success. That's the reality. But recognize this: If you never even launch your syndicated show in the first place, you're an automatic failure. Action is the number one thing that separates the winners from losers in this business (as in every other business).

Chapter 19 – Starting Your Own Network

After reading this far, we sincerely hope you realize that it's possible not only to syndicate yourself in the medium of your choice, but also to reach a mass audience—while earning an income. All you have to do is follow the right steps, take a strategic approach, and be very persistent.

But if the idea of syndication still seems slightly farfetched to you, prepare to enter a whole new dimension of disbelief. In this chapter, we are going to lay out what we consider to be the achievable and worthwhile goal of creating and growing your own successful syndication network.

What's the Point?

For most readers, syndicating their own product to a mass audience will be fulfilling enough. But like tends to attract like. As you proceed with syndication of your content, you will encounter others who share the same passionate interest in whatever your favorite niche topic may be.

Some may also be interested in creating content, but they may be waiting for a flash of inspiration to get them started. Others may already be producing topical content, perhaps in a less widely distributed form than yours (such as a blog or email newsletter). Still others may actually be syndicating their content in the same niche as yours, or in a related one.

Here lies the potential to pull these disparate voices together into one cohesive syndication network.

Let us make a syntactic point here about our use of the term *network*. When any syndicated product is distributed to local outlets, it is effectively on a network—a network that consists of its multiple points of distribution. But in this chapter, we are talking about a larger type of network, one that distributes multiple products and has the potential for even wider distribution.

A Network Is a Business

Our company is called Syndication Networks Corp. for a logical reason—that's exactly what it is: a series of networks that consist of syndicated products. There are also advertising opportunities attached to each network. Let us explain.

Each radio show we syndicate has its own network of station affiliates, and its own set of advertising avails. For example, if an advertiser wants to buy spots in a certain sports show, we sell them spots in that show. The spots then air on the sports show's network of stations.

But we can also sell ads to a single advertiser in multiple radio shows, simultaneously. We do this by combining a group of smaller networks into one larger network. These larger networks meet the requirements for advertisers with bigger needs and budgets. Being part of a larger network also helps our clients, who benefit from large-scale opportunities they would have missed with their shows sold only as individual products.

Years ago, our company entered the Internet radio space with a handful of online talk shows. Today we stream dozens and dozens of different shows, and our on-demand library consists of tens of thousands of hours of content, all at TalkZone.com. Each of the online products has revenue opportunities attached to it, as does the entire, combined network of Internet shows. Thus, our Internet radio show hosts can benefit from ad avails sold in their own shows, as well as from ads sold across our entire Internet radio network.

There are many noble reasons why a media business may exist. A media business may enlighten and inspire millions. It can help make the world a better place. But the most basic purpose of any business is to earn a profit. Simply put, owning a network can mean more income opportunities for you than a stand-alone syndicated product.

You can partner with an existing network or syndication company to take advantage of larger income opportunities. Or, if you have greater resources to invest and a longer term vision, you can consider launching your own network.

Other Benefits of a Network

Aside from greater income opportunities, a network can present a unified voice with a major presence in your chosen niche. For example, let's say you host a partisan political talk show. Your show itself may have some impact. But when your show is combined with a dozen (or several dozen) shows in a similar genre, the resulting chorus of voices can be startlingly powerful and cohesive.

Using the example we just mentioned, let's say an opponent tried to squelch a syndicated talk-show host by launching a direct attack on them in the mainstream media. A frontal assault like that might readily put that talk host on the defensive. But it's far more difficult for someone to intimidate an entire network.

A network can act somewhat like a fortress in the media landscape, protecting its individual hosts. Of course, a network can be attacked, too, but its relative size makes it a more formidable foe than a single host.

Another benefit of a network is its ability to build a large library of content over time, assuming all participants agree to cooperate in this way. A large archive library can be used to attract a larger total audience, to increase search-engine traffic, to offer on-demand content, and to generate additional revenue.

There are also economies of scale within a network, especially in the critical areas of marketing and distribution. A single distribution platform can serve all the participants, at a much lower cost per product.

Creating a Network

What does it take to build a network? Simply put, it requires most of the same things needed to syndicate a single product:

- Marketing to build a list of local media outlets
- Distribution system for the network content
- Brand name and brand image
- A way to monetize the results

In fact, the only key difference between one syndicated product and a network is that the network has multiple products. That means that the syndication of your product and just one additional product on the same distribution channel can legitimately be called a network.

Multimedia Offerings

There's no reason why a network has to limit its products to one medium. In other words, your network doesn't have to distribute only radio shows, or only print content, or only TV shows. You can offer your affiliates content in multimedia form.

Consider the top media networks, for example. The Big Four OTA (over-the-air) TV networks also distribute content to cable, the Internet, and (in some cases) radio. Cable TV network ESPN is also very active in radio and online.

Syndicated content distributed on the Web can easily be offered in multimedia form, such as text, audio, video, or all three.

Distribution Factors to Consider

One hurdle to network creation is designing, funding, and building a content distribution system capable of rapid expansion, ad insertion, content archiving, and other key functions. And if a 24/7 live network is desired, a full-featured production and distribution system can become quite costly to build.

For broadcast radio and television, the complex network infrastructure required to deliver live, 24/7 content goes beyond the scope of this book. Expert technical advice is needed to accomplish this ambitious goal.

Internet Media Network

With the Internet, the situation is different from traditional broadcasting. A professional online multimedia network can be operated by one individual in the beginning. As it grows, duties can easily be shifted to others. A well-designed Web network can stream live audio and/or video around the clock, while offering visitors 24/7 on-demand distribution, text and image descriptions, audio and video ads, pre-roll video ads, ad banners, blogging capabilities, site membership functions, and more.

The owner of an Internet multimedia network can realize income in a number of ways. These include paid advertising of specific content, ongoing site-wide advertising, fees paid to the network by the participants as shared cost, monetization of the archive library, membership dues, and other revenue sources.

A disclaimer and a modest plug are appropriate here. Our company markets an Internet media distribution platform called RadioCommand. An example of a media site powered by this platform is TalkZone.com. If this idea intrigues you, you can watch a free video tour of the RadioCommand platform at www.radiocommand.com.

A number of online media networks provide distribution of individual audio or video products, and/or clusters of topic-related products. Some also offer free streaming and podcast delivery.

However, these sites cannot provide all the different income possibilities that a privately owned network can. Many such sites are also moving to restrict bandwidth, cut back on stream quality, or charge fees for distribution.

If you currently use an online network for distribution, the cost squeeze may be another reason to consider starting your own network. Why pay someone else for content distribution, when others could pay YOU, as the owner of a network?

Whatever distribution system you choose, a robust and battle-tested platform will likely be more affordable and more reliable long-term than trying to build something from scratch.

Internet Content Network

The so-called Internet content network is another variation to consider. We've previously described sites that aggregate articles about different topics, in order to make the site rank high in search engines and generate visitor traffic. The traffic is then converted into profits through ads and other forms of monetization. Although recent refinements by major search engines have impacted the rankings of these sites, many still pull lots of traffic.

As we've mentioned, you can contribute content to such sites and earn modest compensation for doing so. But there's nothing stopping you—other than time and effort—from building your very own Internet content network, or even a series of networks.

If you go this route, one option is to focus an entire site on one particular niche subject. Most of the large content networks cover a range of topics, so being more specific will help your site stand out in its niche.

What Goes into a Content Site?

The primary ingredients you will need for a content site are as follows:

- A searchable, SEO–optimized, and easy-to-navigate site design
- An RSS feed, so subscribers can track any new site additions
- An ongoing supply of content

You can solicit content from providers at large, either as free editorial contributions or on a paid basis. You can commission articles from writers you hire. You can even buy an existing library of content.

You might wish to consider posting content of a timeless nature, such as 'how-to' advice, rather than articles that quickly become dated. The timeless approach may prove more logical over the long run, since your content will retain value for readers and your site can better attract ongoing traffic.

We've only touched on the possibilities of network ownership in this chapter. This approach to syndication may be one to consider, if the idea of partnering with other content providers in your niche appeals to you.

Chapter 20 – Syndication Nation

Listening to music of virtually all kinds is something that we enjoy. So it's an everyday thing to be grooving to music from a variety of sources: broadcast radio, smartphone, satellite radio, a web stream, mp3 player, laptop files, and so on. Not to mention live performances, when we manage to get tickets.

Of course, all that music listening competes with other media content, such as talk shows, sports broadcasts, and more.

Jukebox Saturday Night

There's another listening habit we'll admit to—reserved for occasional times. Over the years, we've managed to collect several well-preserved jukeboxes from the 1940s and 1950s.

It's always fun to watch their whirling displays of color and light. The mechanism behind the glass selects the disc, gently sets it on the turntable, and the needle drops into the groove. The sound is rich and full. And the cabinets are like works of art, with polished hardwood and gleaming chrome.

What does a small collection of jukeboxes have to do with syndication? Well, here's the story. Back in the mid-20th century, classic jukeboxes like mine were found in countless restaurants, bars, and other public places. They were just considered part of the scenery.

But today, most who see these classic jukes in action are dazzled by them. Modern jukebox designs are bland and boring in comparison.

Jukebox collectors now refer to the 1940s as the Golden Age of Jukeboxes, and the 1950s as the Silver Age. Yet back when these machines were in common use, few thought of them as exceptional.

An Invisible Golden Era

Now here's the point to the jukebox story.

Human beings seem to be exceptionally poor at recognizing a golden age when it's in progress. We can assure you, nobody in the mid to late 1940s was saying "We're living in the Golden Age of Jukeboxes!"

Golden ages of peace and prosperity occur periodically in history. While they're in progress, most everyone just takes them for granted. People assume the good times will last forever.

Then, when the golden age inevitably becomes history, everyone suddenly wishes they had taken better advantage of the windows of opportunity that they missed—opportunities they assumed would be around forever.

Ah, the Good Old Days

Let us suggest something you may not have considered. We believe all of us are now living in the Golden Age of Syndication.

We've dealt with radio syndicators for over three decades, beginning with the early career days as a program director. Those folks would regularly phone me to pitch their syndicated shows. We had many a conversation over the years that went something like this:

Yours Truly: "So how are things going with your show?"

Syndicator: "Good, but I sure wish we'd launched this thing five or ten years ago. Things today are tough. Back then, stations seemed open to taking new shows. Now it's a real challenge."

We first recall hearing a comment like this around 1982. Back then, we were usually sympathetic. We'd say something like, "Yes, things must be tough for you these days." Although we didn't quite know why that would be the case.

Around 1990, we remember speaking to somebody else who was pitching us on another syndicated show. During the conversation, we asked how it was going for them. The reply was eerily similar to what we'd heard almost a decade before: "To be honest, I wish we'd launched the show years ago. Syndication was so much easier then!" This time, I tried not to chuckle.

In the 1990s, while successfully syndicating *The Success Journal*, we founded our syndication consulting company. At that time, we received several friendly but slightly concerned messages from people we knew in the media. One cautioned us that syndication wasn't the piece of cake it had been a few years earlier, back around 1990!

Another suggested we were taking a risk, trying to launch a syndication firm during such a challenging era (there was a recession at the time). We listened politely and then went ahead with our plans. Despite the naysayers, our company had immediate growth. Within a couple of years we moved to larger offices, build additional studio space, and hired more staff.

As the first decade of the 2000s rolled by, our company continued to expand. Periodically we'd speak to various longtime syndicators. They usually had a nostalgic word or two about the "days of yore." Once we even heard this sentiment from one of our staff members, whom we quickly set straight.

Perhaps it's human nature to always long for the good old days, but for some reason this thinking seems rampant in the syndication biz.

The point is that even the so-called experts are poor judges of true market conditions.

"If only I'd started then" seems to be an endless mindset. Our belief, borne out by actual results, is that there's no time like the present to begin. And no matter when you start, you'll always wish you'd started sooner!

Now's the Best Time

We firmly believe that the present—right now—happens to be the best time in modern history to launch a syndicated media product, with the greatest chance of success in reaching a mass audience. It's the second decade of the 2000s, and we are living in THE Golden Age of Syndication. If you want to join the Syndication Nation, we consider this the best time ever to do so.

We're willing to bet that folks will one day look back on this time window and say, "If only I'd started THEN!" But instead of blowing smoke, they'll be stating an irrefutable fact.

The following are six reasons why we believe this to be true.

1. Traditional media remain strong, despite digital media inroads.

At present, many millions of consumers remain loyal to the older, established forms of media. For example, in the case of broadcast radio, studies indicate that listeners will remain loyal to traditional radio for AT LEAST the next 10 years, after which digital media is expected to cause audience erosion. (According to a study by Bridge Ratings, in-car Web listening will by then surpass over-the-air listening.)

Right now there's still a huge window of opportunity to syndicate to traditional media and enjoy the many benefits. Traditional media offer an ideal place to establish a mass national audience. Once established, you can later transfer your audience dominance to digital media (which has far more fragmentation than traditional media).

2. Technological barriers are falling fast.

The production quality edge once enjoyed by top media professionals is receding. Almost anyone can now create top-quality, professional media content at low cost. For example, sophisticated video editing software now runs under $100. Just a few years ago, a studio and crew were needed for similar results.

The main barrier to cheap, high-quality content is the learning curve required to use the software. At present, you can remain ahead of the pack, since most people are held back by the slightly complex learning curve.

But we expect that fully automated tools for creating masterful media will soon be everywhere. This is simply the inevitable progression of technology.

When that day arrives, the bar will be considerably lowered. So this may be the ideal time to take advantage of superior technical quality for your content, before pro-level quality gets in the hands of everyman.

3. The consolidation process continues in traditional media.

Consolidation means fewer and fewer corporations now own more and more local media outlets. Since most big firms are publicly traded, they focus on short-term results. Hence, local budgets remain tight. This squeeze has opened the door wide for more syndicated content to fill the gap at low cost. In fact, we believe this is one big reason we're in the Golden Age of Syndication.

But nothing lasts forever! Local management's autonomy may suddenly vanish. For example, a corporation may decide to vertically integrate (produce its own content). Then, doors will start closing to new syndicated products. Even if this happens, established syndicated content that is delivering results will likely be retained. Few local outlets would ever remove proven content that is giving them audience and revenue.

You still have time to establish yourself and build an audience, while doors to local outlets remain wide open.

4. There are more channels hungry for media content than ever before.

When you consider digital online media, digital TV channels, mobile media, Web streaming, the imminent arrival of the digital car dashboard, and all the rest, we're still in the Wild West days of digital media. In some ways, the present digital/mobile media jumble resembles the early days of the Web, when there was a literal gold rush underway. Some jumped into the fray, planted a flag, and eventually became fabulously wealthy. Others did not. But countless opportunities were there for Web pioneers.

We view today's digital media landscape in a similar way. Entrepreneurs are leaping in, while larger, slower moving companies are still trying to figure out what to do. What better time to secure a digital foothold for your syndicated content? You have time now to dominate a profitable media niche, or even launch your own syndication network (see Chapter 19).

5. One irrefutable fact is that all economies go through cycles.

We'll try not to bore you with this point. At present, the U.S. economy is in a mixed mode, with money tight for most people. So you might assume now is not the best time to launch a syndication project.

Actually, we believe the opposite to be true.

A slower economy takes pressure off local ad inventory, meaning local outlets have room for barter spots. An uncertain economy also has people sitting on the sidelines, waiting for better days. This means that your marketing can have a far bigger impact during this time. Eventually, the business cycle will accelerate, and present opportunities will be lost.

6. Two words: affordable distribution.

Just a few years ago, one of the top-line costs at any network or syndication company was the huge expense of content delivery. In the case of our company, we had to burn, imprint, and ship out thousands of compact discs, track sheets, affidavits, and other material to stations on a regular basis. Not only were all those CDs, documents, printing supplies, envelopes, and shipping charges very costly, but the process required lots of time and labor every week.

Today, it costs remarkably little to digitally distribute the very same content to the nearly 2,000 affiliate stations we serve. We continue to distribute certain programs via satellite, and this technology has advanced in recent years. TV syndication also uses digital systems for program delivery to stations. Easier, faster, more affordable distribution is another reason we're in the Golden Age of Syndication.

If six reasons aren't enough to convince you this is the Golden Age, we can give you a few more:

- A vibrant 24/7 media cycle, constantly demanding fresh content
- Today's faster speed-to-market for new syndicated products
- Quicker, easier product launch process

We're All Connected

One proven way to achieve any result is to follow the trailblazers. Meet, greet, and network with others in the same field. One sharp idea from an expert can revolutionize the way you view things. In fact, there's often a better way to do most anything—you just have to learn what it is. Knowledge and information, plus expert advice when you need it, will help get you past the roadblocks.

How to Begin

After you finish reading this chapter, we invite you to do just one thing. Take out a sheet of paper and at the top of the page write your ultimate syndication goal. In other words, what ideal result do you hope to achieve by syndicating your content?

Don't worry about making it perfect at this point. No one is meant to read this goal but you. Just start writing what comes to mind. You can always change it later.

For now, we simply want you to capture the moment on paper. There is real energy in grabbing the present MOMENT and turning it into MOMENTUM, to help you move ahead with your plans.

Below your ultimate syndication goal or goals, write down the very first steps you will need to take to get moving and to start fulfilling your dream. Again, there's no need to be perfect here. Just jot down some steps to get you started toward that goal. You can break these initial steps down into tiny ones, if you wish.

Doing, Doing, Done

If you can achieve just one of these steps each day, in one week you will have made real progress. In one month, you will be farther along the path than you can now imagine.

But don't stop there. You'll eventually want to jot down every step you can think of in the syndication process, such as choosing the type of content you will create, deciding which medium you favor (radio, TV, Web, etc.), honing the specific niche topic you will address, defining the type of audience will you serve, and so on.

Other steps might involve creating samples of your content, setting up a budget, learning more about marketing and distribution, planning to attend a convention, finding a mentor or advisor, building a website, and so on.

272

Keep up this step-by-step process and watch how far you get after 90 days, six months, and one year down the road!

There's a Nation Out There

Along the way, you can network, gather info, and adjust your plans for maximum effectiveness. Success in syndication, like any worthwhile goal in life, will call for you to remain persistent and not let yourself become discouraged by the inevitable ups and downs.

There are no guarantees in life, of course, and there are none in syndication. But if you can create worthy content that an audience finds compelling, and you follow the proven steps taken by others, eventually you can experience the thrill of seeing your ultimate syndication goals become reality.

Why wait another minute to begin? There's no better time than this very moment for you to become part of the Syndication Nation.

Glossary of Terms

Affiliate: A broadcast station that is part of your network. Or, may be used to describe an online sales referral partner.

Arbitron: A company specializing in radio and online audience ratings and research.

Audit Bureau of Circulations: A company specializing in print circulation and readership research.

Barter: Much of radio and TV syndication operates on a barter commercial basis, where ad inventory is bartered (traded) for content.

BEP: Back-end profits which may be generated over time by a syndicated product, after its initial exposure.

Content Farm: Used to describe a website which aggregates content, usually created by a number of contributors.

CM3: Critical Mass to Make Money (see Critical Mass)

CPA: Cost Per Action or Cost Per Acquisition. An online advertiser pays for an action taken from an ad.

CPC: Cost Per Click. Payment is made when an ad is clicked.

CPL: Cost Per Lead. Payment is made for each lead provided.

Critical Mass Audience: The audience threshold at which a syndicated product can reliably be sold to national advertisers.

Distributor: Term used in TV syndication to describe a company that manages the show distribution to stations.

EI: Entertainment and Information content, usually children's programming, in TV syndication.

First-Run Syndication: In TV syndication, this term refers to shows which air for the first time as syndicated products, as opposed to Off-Network Syndication.

Full Content Syndication: In online syndication, refers to distribution of the entire product to subscribers, as opposed to Partial Content Syndication.

Independent Networks: Broadcast networks which are not owned by a large corporation or affiliated with a wired network, as opposed to Traditional Networks.

M + E Track: In TV syndication, a separate audio track containing music and effects for easier foreign dubbing.

MIPTV, MIPCOM: International TV content trade shows where TV syndicators showcase their products.

NAB: National Association of Broadcasters. The NAB hosts its conventions in the Spring and Fall.

NATPE: National Association of Television Program Executives. NATPE hosts a large annual TV convention.

Neilsen: A company specializing in television audience ratings and research.

News Feed: See Web Feed.

Partial Content Syndication: In online syndication, refers to distribution of a tease or headline to subscribers, as opposed to Full Content Syndication.

Per Inquiry: In broadcast syndication, advertising in which payment is made for each lead that is generated by the ad.

Pay Per Call: A similar broadcast ad model to Per Inquiry.

Off-Network: In TV syndication, refers to content that first aired on a network and is later syndicated to stations.

OTA: In TV syndication, refers to Over The Air broadcast signals, as opposed to cable networks.

ROS: In broadcast advertising, Run Of Schedule refers to ads scheduled to air at various times chosen by the broadcaster. In online advertising, Run Of Site refers to ads which appear on various web pages chosen by the site owner.

RSS: Really Simply Syndication. This term describes a popular online subscription model of content distribution.

Self-Syndication: Syndication which is undertaken by a content creator.

Traditional Network: A network with a large corporate ownership, and possibly a large wired network (as opposed to an Independent Network).

Viral Syndication: Grassroots online syndication which takes on a life of its own, hence the viral connotation.

Web Feed: A subscription model of online distribution which offers users frequently updated content. Also referred to as a News Feed.

Web Syndication: A form of online distribution in which the content of one website is offered to other websites.

Index

May We Be Of Service To You?

Syndication Networks Corp. (SNC) is a leader in radio syndication. We have been in business for over 20 years, with offices and studios in the Chicago area. Our shows are heard on 2,000 radio stations across North America. Our staff has over 150 years of combined experience in broadcasting and syndication.

SNC welcomes the challenge of syndicating newer, start-up, or relatively unproven shows to the radio industry. We can also accelerate the growth of existing syndicated shows. Our staffing and infrastructure are designed to have excess capacity, allowing us to capably manage our roster of established shows, along with a number of newer, unproven shows, all on an equal footing.

SNC will expertly market your show to the radio industry. We will deliver your show to stations via XDS satellite or FTP download. And we will manage your show's advertising sales, invoicing, payments, and all other network services.

If you're a content creator who wants to syndicate, or your syndicated show isn't growing as fast as it should, we'd be delighted to hear from you. Visit the link below to learn more.

Please note, this offer is not for everyone.

1. We only accept a limited number of shows for syndication.
2. Some shows will not fit our company portfolio.

Take The First Step Now. Login and Learn More at

www.SyndicationInfo.com